QOHELETH

Continental Commentaries

Old Testament

Genesis 1–11, Genesis 12–36, Genesis 37–50
Claus Westermann

Psalms 1–59
Hans-Joachim Kraus

Psalm 60–150
Hans-Joachim Kraus

Theology of the Psalms
Hans-Joachim Kraus

The Song of Songs
Othmas Keel

Isaiah 1–12, Isaiah 13–27, Isaiah 28–39
Hans Wildberger

Obadiah and Jonah
Hans Walter Wolff

Micah
Hans Walter Wolff

Haggai
Hans Walter Wolff

* * * *

New Testament

Matthew 1–7
Ulrich Luz

Galatians
Dieter Lührmann

Revelation
Jürgen Roloff

NORBERT LOHFINK

QOHELETH

A Continental Commentary

Translated by
Sean McEvenue

FORTRESS PRESS
MINNEAPOLIS

QOHELETH
A Continental Commentary

Copyright © 2003 Augsburg Fortress. All rights reserved. Except for brief quotations in critical articles or reviews, no part of this book may be reproduced in any manner without prior written permission from the publisher. Write: Permissions, Augsburg Fortress, Box 1209, Minneapolis, MN 55440.

Translated and revised from the German edition, published as *Kohelet,* Die neue Echter Bibel, (Würzburg: Echter Verlag, 1980). Translated with the author's permission.

Scripture quotations are the author's and translator's translations.

Library of Congress Cataloging-in-Publication Data

Lohfink, Norbert.
  [Kohelet. English]
  Qoheleth : a Continental commentary / Norbert Lohfink ; translated by
Sean McEvenue.
    p. cm. — (Continental commentaries)
Includes bibliographical references and index.
  ISBN 0-8006-9604-2 (hardcover : alk. paper)
  1. Bible. O.T. Ecclesiastes—Commentaries. I. Title. II. Series.
BS1475.53.L6413 2002
223'.8077—dc21

                                              2002152638

The paper used in this publication meets the minimum requirements of American National Standard for Information Sciences — Permanence of Paper for Printed Library Materials, ANSI Z329.48-1984.

Printed in Canada
07   06   05   04   03   1   2   3   4   5   6   7   8   9   10

Contents

Contents

Preface

I am very pleased that Fortress Press has offered me the means to make my Qoheleth commentary available in English translation. It first appeared in 1980 and has gone through five German printings. But still I very much approve the publication of an English version. It introduces new aspects to the interpretation of Qoheleth, aspects that even now in the most recent Qoheleth commentary literature are not to be found in consolidated form. Also other commentaries about to be published in the near future, notably the one by Thomas Krüger in the Hermeneia series, frequently refer readers to my commentary, in which case it is helpful for English-speaking readers to be able to consult it.

My commentary is not in the form of an academic commentary. I was made responsible for the book of Qoheleth on the team that produced the *Deutsche Einheitsübersetzung* between 1960 and 1980. The work of translation stretched out in time, and I was repeatedly fascinated by new discoveries I was making in this very special book of the Bible, discoveries that did not reach adequate expression in earlier translations. In this way there arose a text that was quite untraditional among German Bible translations. The *Einheitsübersetzung* has, in the interim, become one of the most commonly used Bible translations in the German language. My commentary is, in some degree, the "commentary of the translator" to the Qoheleth translation itself. I wrote it just as the translation came to completion and was published. For the German users of the *Einheitsübersetzung,* I wanted to explain more clearly everything contained in this wonderfully expressive biblical book. I was not thinking of professors as my readers. I made no footnotes and did not enter into discussions with other commentaries, books, or articles. All of that I have done in a series of scholarly articles, which are indicated in the bibliography. The commentary is in some way the bridge between the translation and the academic research papers. Absolutely indispensable for it is the new English translation that Sean McEvenue has competently prepared, based on the original Hebrew text but taking the lead from my German translation. It is in itself the first half of the interpretation. To use this commentary properly, one must move back and forth between the translation and the commentary.

With twenty years of perspective, I reflect on what new contribution to Qoheleth interpretation this translation and commentary have made. First is the new awareness of the literary form of the book. Qoheleth was not sufficiently seen as literature. As a student I was introduced to that school of literary criticism called the "New Criticism" in England and North America. I learned to pay attention to the concrete form of the text and its structures much more than the previous generation had. In this context, it was especially important for me that the apparent contradictions in the Book of Qoheleth often resulted from the fact that the author was citing the ideas of others or was playing upon them. A second point was that I was enabled to free myself from the notion that Qoheleth's discussion was exclusively with the wisdom teachers of Israel and their books, notably Proverbs. I came to the (ancient, and long-forgotten) conviction that Qoheleth undertook to dispute with a broader, international wisdom, Hellenistic wisdom. To dispute with it, he appropriated it and directly criticized it on the basis of his biblical tradition. It probably had marked not only his thought but also his lifestyle. He seems to have been a peripatetic philosopher; he walked about in Palestine, and he taught in Hebrew, not in Greek. A third aspect is closely linked with that fact: my effort to sketch the form of Qoheleth against the background of what we know about the economic and social situation of Ptolomaic Palestine. Clearly Qoheleth belongs to the upper echelons of Jewish society in Jerusalem, and he writes for that class. Finally, a fourth element is my discovery early on of something others were also finding at the same time and soon thereafter: the astonishing proximity of Qoheleth's thought to modern existential philosophy. I had been introduced to this as well in my early years, because it dominated European thought during my student years. Other colleagues have invoked especially Albert Camus as a comparable figure. For my part, I found that the writings of Karl Jaspers were most helpful. These four elements together probably formed a constellation that made something new out of my Qoheleth commentary.

I do not claim in any way that this commentary contains only new and original material. There are so many people to whom I am grateful for so much—exegetes from earlier generations like C. D. Ginsburg

(1861) and L. Levy (1912), but just as many colleagues of my own generation. I have also taken much inspiration from the American sphere. The observations concerning language, style, and structure were sparked through a meeting with Addison G. Wright in a seminar at the meeting of the Catholic Biblical Association in 1969. In it we discussed his paper "The Riddle of the Sphinx." This reactivated my earlier experiences with the New Criticism. Nevertheless, I took a position very distant from his, regarding the structure of the book. For the insight that Qoheleth often cites or plays upon the texts of his adversaries, I thank especially the commentary of R. Gordis, which I still consider to be one of the best commentaries ever written on Qoheleth (*Koheleth: The Man and His World,* 1951). It was my professor in Rome, Mitchell Dahood, who freed me from the constriction of looking only to traditional Israelite wisdom. He extended my horizon to Phoenicia, and from there to the Greeks was not far. Still I needed much time and effort to break away from his much-too-careless treatment of the received text, and through this work it also became progressively more evident to me that Qoheleth is to be dated in the Hellenistic period. Very important for me, in this regard, was the book of R. Braun concerning *Kohelet und die frühhellenistische Popularphilosophie* (1973). Concerning the political, economic, and social world of Qoheleth, I learned most of all from the books of M. Rostovzeff, which I first read in their original English editions. In my categorizing Qoheleth as a precursor of existential philosophy, I was confirmed by the first Qoheleth commentary of Michael V. Fox (1989), which came too late for the first edition of my commentary, but which gave me some ideas for the revision. This, then, leads me to the next topic. But first I would like simply to summarize and underline how much I have written this commentary in contact with American exegesis.

My German publisher was not able to permit me a revision of the whole commentary, despite repeated printings. I had prepared one in 1990 or thereabouts. I have provided my revised version now for the English edition. So this English translation is now a new, and henceforth the only, authentic version. Since the revision, another ten years have passed. Unfortunately, however, I was unable to make a subsequent revision once again, in order to include the very latest results of Qoheleth research. But that is possibly a good thing. In recent years a lot of new and intensive work on Qoheleth has been underway. Probably, in a further revision, my commentary would have an entirely new face. But it seems to me be better for the Continental Commentary series that it should appear there essentially in its first form, and say the word it had to say to its time.

Preface

I had great pleasure in working with Dr. Sean McEvenue, the translator. Several emails often crossed the ocean in a single day. It was very hard work to translate the text of Qoheleth anew from the Hebrew and to pay attention to all the nuances of my own translation and commentary. He also added the exact references of the non-biblical quotations, which were missing in the German original. I would like to thank him now for all his work from my heart.

Frankfurt am Main
September 7, 2002

Translator's Note

It has been an honor to be invited to make this book available to English readers, and also a major challenge—an honor because I have believed for years that this book makes a profound and illuminating contribution to our understanding of the Bible; a challenge because, beyond the expected difficulty of expressing in English the complex nested logical thought that German grammar facilitates and favors, there is the razor-edge precision of Dr. Lohfink's understanding and writing, which demands very attentive work in every sentence.

The book, after the introduction, first gives the running text of the translation, to enable an unconnected reading before or after studying the commentary. Then it presents its materials in five different formats: a translation of the biblical book, some text-critical observations in endnotes after the translation, cross-references in the margins, the running commentary, and non-biblical parallels in footnotes to the commentary. The biblical text itself I have translated directly from the Hebrew, while taking care to follow the direction and exegetical decisions in each case of Dr. Lohfink's German translation. The translation and the running commentary are very much in dialogue with each other, so the commentary reader is strongly advised to work, not with whatever biblical translation is most familiar, but directly with this translation.

The cross-references are particularly helpful. Qoheleth has been seen as an original and idiosyncratic writer. But recent scholarship has begun to reveal the intimate dependence of his text on his biblical tradition. The references provided in the margins and the contexts they imply are generally not discussed in the running commentary, but they do provide the reader with an initial basis for making those connections. They reveal Qoheleth as "the head of a household who brings from his storeroom both the new and the old." The following sigla are used in the cross-references:

+   a plus sign indicates that the cross-reference is the main text for this idea; additional marginal references will be found at this text

|| two parallel vertical lines indicate a real parallel with similar
      wording

⟋   an arrow indicates that the marginal cross-reference is a quotation
      of or an allusion to the present text in a later book of the Bible

no siglum with a cross-reference indicates that something interesting will
      be found in this text

The running commentary is characterized by a method of detailed observation of structure and literary form and a reading against the background of the author's social history as a distinguished Jerusalem scholar in Hellenistic times. Dr. Lohfink has become recognized as a world master in this kind of exegesis over a lifetime of spectacular publication, especially in his work on Deuteronomy. In this commentary on Qoheleth, he uses the most minute observation of word and phrase repetition to lay bare the system of literary structures that any reader may feel underlie this text but that have always seemed too elusive to be described. There results a wonderful dawning of intelligibility that fully rewards the work entailed.

To return to the biblical text, one of the most subtle difficulties Qoheleth has enmeshed in his text are the numerous references to traditional texts familiar to his readers, but often unknown to later centuries. These references are sometimes by way of partial citation (of biblical texts, of his adversaries, and even of his own text) and sometimes by more subtle allusions to familiar modes of thought. Of course the Hebrew manuscripts had no convention of punctuation with quotation marks, let alone footnotes! It is the commentary that indicates such meanings, but it is hoped that the translation takes care not to disturb in English whatever order of words makes such an interpretation possible or likely.

In these cases, and also in many other situations, Qoheleth often moves abruptly from prose to verse or from verse to prose without any signal beyond those very subtle stylistic signals of Hebrew verse. Examples of this can be found on almost any page. The translation indicates these shifts by shifting margins between prose and poetry, and by whatever shifts in grammar and style were justified by the Hebrew text.

It may be helpful, further, to note two systematic constraints, peculiar to the text of Qoheleth, which leave their mark on the translation. First, both the commentary author and the translator are acutely aware that in recent years the meanings of English words have shifted to finally recognize that all human beings are created equal—that "man" no longer conveys the concept of "human," "his" does not mean "his or her," and so forth; nevertheless, English sadly has no single word to correspond to those words in Hebrew, Greek, and other languages that simply denote a human being, without reference to gender. Contemporary English writers have adopted a range of dodges to handle situations in which our linguistic resources are still inadequate—often shifting masculine singular to the plural "their," or moving to the first person plural "we" and "our," where gender is not expressed. Such solutions are frequently not possible in translating Qoheleth. His method of thought seems never to revert to the kind of mutual subjective awareness that comes so easily to us, as if, for example, I should write that we all generalize easily about our individual experience. To translate his third person singular pronouns into first person plurals would be to transpose his thought into something he would not recognize. Moreover, a significant aspect of his method is to oppose the generalizations about humanity found in "traditional" wisdom by adducing a single instance, of a single man, who disproves the tradition. Virgil's "*ab uno disce omnes*"—"in the one understand all of them"—is his kind of empiricism. Where contemporary English would replace Qoheleth's masculine singular with a neutral plural, sometimes you can get away with it, but at other times that small shift would break the whole style, feel, and force of the unit. In such cases, this translation has often used "one" and "one's," reluctantly suffering the stilted character of that usage. Other contexts have allowed it to use "human being." Sometimes it has unhappily remained with the masculine. For example, the "his" in 11:5 seems to be required, not so much by the logic in this case, but by the text's poetic mode and strong feelings: this is very much a contemplation of a single sad moment and not of a generic idea; it is the passing of an individual who is felt though not identified. It may be fictional, but it is not a parable.

The second constraint that marks the translation arises from Qoheleth's use of linkwords and key words to articulate the structure of his text, the logic of his argument, and the connections between his thoughts. All of this is richly documented in the commentary. It needs also to be expressed in the translation of the biblical text. This, of course, runs counter to the linguistic fact that Hebrew offers a small number of words, whereas English offers an incomparable treasure of synonyms with subtle differentiation in meaning, and to the interpreter's principle that the precise meaning of a given word is ultimately determined by immediate context. Moreover, English literary (as opposed to technical) writers will often avoid using the same word twice on the same page, even when precisely the same idea is intended, just as they once avoided using the identical spelling. A translator of Qoheleth has to lay all those English instincts aside, or too much of Qoheleth's meaning will become invisible. At the same time, the chasm between English and Hebrew is such that each case has to be considered separately.

An outstanding example of this is, perhaps, the word *ṭôb,* which means simply "good," but which in context can mean such a variety of precise things: well-being, prosperity, good luck, reward, essential goodness, fruitfulness, blessedness, bliss, happiness, excellence, virtue, moral act, and so forth. Qoheleth uses this word forty-six times. One cannot opt for a totally neutral identical translation such as "good" and rigidly stick with it throughout, because then the word would be a cipher or signal rather than part of language. Conversely one cannot simply choose a different precise word for each context, losing all the structure-signaling functions, because in any case each context looks to neighboring contexts and corresponding contexts, and these often use the same word. In this case, in the opening unit (1:12—3:15) the word occurs eight times. I was able to translate it as "happiness" six times, but had to translate it as "blessed" twice in 2:26. Something of the structuring through repeated words is clearly lost by this, but I could find no way around it that did not do worse damage in terms of loss of meaning. In the whole Qoheleth book the word has been translated as "happiness" sixteen times. Another eighteen times it has been translated as "better" in connection with the familiar figure of proverbs, "better this than that." In 6:12 sticking to the word "better," where most (or perhaps all?) other translations use "good," is very helpful as it serves to clarify what is referred to, that is, the traditional thinking in proverbs. Contexts of the remaining ten occurrences require that they be translated by different words: "prosperity" (four times), "good" (four times), "right" in 7:20, and "reward" in 4:9.

The awkward translation in 4:7, "I further observed a breath," can be justified by the fact that the Hebrew says literally that. Moreover, the word "breath" is a major structuring word throughout the book, and its meaning within the book has become gradually clarified to the point that it serves as a *terminus technicus.* Hence, despite the awkwardness, I have translated this way, preserving Qoheleth's own awkward system of key words and link words.

In 6:2 the word "eat" is not normally associated with wealth, holdings, and honor. It has occurred, however, in 5:10, 11, 16, 17, 18, and now twice in this verse. Clearly it has acquired a special role, establishing a metaphor within which all else is held together, and also signaling that the unit of 6:1-10 is linked with what precedes. This motivates a translation that fails to fit the immediate context but retains a general context. An alternative would be to use an abstract word such as "consume," and I have taken that route in 5:18 where the whole sentence tends to the abstract. But the use of "consume" in 5:18 makes it all the more urgent to restore the ongoing metaphor by repeating "eat" in 6:2.

Any translation cannot fail to be a disappointment to those who know the original and grasp it in so many different dimensions. I hope that these few observations, and the examples provided, may clarify some concerns of the translator and serve to explain some otherwise puzzling characteristics of the translation.

Lafayette, Louisiana
September 9, 2002

Abbreviations

AB	Anchor Bible
ABD	*Anchor Bible Dictionary.* Edited by D. N. Freedman. 6 vols. New York, 1992
ABR	*Australian Biblical Review*
ANET	J. B. Pritchard, ed., *Ancient Near Eastern Texts Relating to the Old Testament,* 3d ed., 1969
ATD	Das Alte Testament Deutsch
BETL	Bibliotheca ephemeridum theologicarum lovaniensium
Bib	*Biblica*
BiKi	*Bibel und Kirche*
BK	Biblischer Kommentar
BTB	*Biblical Theology Bulletin*
BZAW	Beihefte zur Zeitschrift für die alttestamentliche Wissenschaft
CBQ	*Catholic Biblical Quarterly*
EtB	Études Bibliques
ExpT	*Expository Times*
FOTL	Forms of the Old Testament Literature
GuL	*Geist und Leben*
HBS	Herders Biblische Studien
HUCA	*Hebrew Union College Annual*
IBC	Interpretation: A Bible Commentary for Teaching and Preaching
Int	*Interpretation*
JAAR	*Journal of the American Academy of Religion*
JBL	*Journal of Biblical Literature*
JSOT	*Journal for the Study of the Old Testament*
JSOTSup	Journal for the Study of the Old Testament: Supplement Series
KAT	Kommentar zum Alten Testament
LCL	Loeb Classical Library
MT	Masoretic text
NCBC	New Century Bible Commentary

Abbreviations

NICOT	New International Commentary on the Old Testament
NRSV	New Revised Standard Version
NT	New Testament
Numen	*Numen: International Review for the History of Religions*
OBO	Orbis biblicus et orientalis
OT	Old Testament
OTG	Old Testament Guides
OTL	Old Testament Library
OTM	Old Testament Message
PSB	*Princeton Seminary Bulletin*
SBAB	Stuttgarter biblische Aufsatzbände
VT	*Vetus Testamentum*
WBC	Word Biblical Commentary
ZAW	*Zeitschrift für die alttestamentliche Wissenschaft*

Introduction

In synagogues the book of Qoheleth is read during the celebration of the Feast of Booths, no doubt because of its invitation to rejoice. Thomas à Kempis took the first sentence in the book—*vanitas vanitatum, omnia vanitas*—as an invitation to despise all earthly things and to desire only the otherworldly. And he was not alone in this. Christian piety has heard mostly this message in the book for over a thousand years. For many modern agnostics this book is the last bridge to the Bible. Some Christians today find in Qoheleth a kind of back door—at once sinister and highly esteemed—through which their minds can admit those skeptical and melancholy sentiments that would be refused entry at portals where cultivation of virtue and belief in the afterlife are inscribed on the lintel.

What is the real message of this book? It presents itself as a teacher's text, and so classifies itself as "wisdom literature." Even the few apparent references to what is contemporary to the author do not obscure the clear basic intent to pronounce timeless truth. From the beginning, its inquiry is about humankind in general. Israel as a nation is put into the background. Moreover, the book is systematically structured.

Survey of the Contents

Qoheleth—for that is the name given to the voice that fills almost the whole book—begins, after a few introductory sentences, by sketching a *cosmology* (1:4-11). The solid earth is the eternal stage upon which the equally eternal other elements of the world gloriously repeat their performance without using themselves up. Only humans come and go; and humans, of course, are the ones who elevate the world to its highest estate by giving it meaning, through their senses, their language, and the accumulating power of their memory. But humans have never kept up with its overwhelming multiplicity. Each generation must rebuild its store of knowledge, because each death wipes it out.

Introduction

Quite logically there follows an *anthropology*, with a theological ending (1:12—3:15). Qoheleth tells a tale presenting himself at the peak of human aspiration. He is a highly educated, technically all-competent shaker and mover, a master of life's pleasures. He tries everything: all prosperity is within the power of humankind. From this perspective he asks about the meaning of all he achieves, and there death shows its face, awaiting each person. In its shadow every ability and every success is seen to be a "puff of breath." This leads only to "despair." In like manner the unpredictability of human decisions, and of the many other factors that determine situations and outcomes, leads to the same conclusion. In theological terms this means that prosperity too is itself given to humans as a gift from God, and is not an assured product of their efforts. Everything that happens is an act of God, and for that reason it is something "perfect." Humans do not perceive this, however, because the sum total of the world is hidden from their eyes. So the human lot is to accept in the "fear of God" whatever God gives.

This grasp of the human condition, drawn as it is from the heights of human achievements, is then shown to be all the more true in a *social critique* section, in which the world is seen as it really is (3:16—6:10). Corruption in the practice of justice, exploitation of the lower classes, unbridled rivalry among the wealthy, isolation of the powerful, unstable popular opinion, self-entangled bureaucracies, bankruptcies, enslavement of formerly propertied persons—in this, the anthropology of "puff of breath" and of "fear of God" is repeatedly validated.

Conversely, those views of the world that had been widely held in former times are now shown to be false. This is the burden of the subsequent section of *deconstruction*, which can be designated as a *refutatio* in the categories of classical rhetoric (6:11—9:6). In ten carefully selected citations the major themes of classical wisdom teaching are proposed and in each case refuted. At the end, it is all about the most basic worldview of classical wisdom: good behavior leads to fortune and long life; bad behavior to misfortune and early death. Insofar as anyone fully understands this principle, one could get a handle on one's future through one's own behavior, and make everything turn out precisely to one's benefit. Qoheleth argues that the facts do not bear this out. Thus humankind is reduced to living each moment and accepting good and evil from God's hand, until death occurs to end it all. After death there is nothing further. So we should sometimes observe the traditional rules for living, and sometimes we should not. Only the "fear of God" can guide us well in

2

making decisions. This will lead to joy as well, when God chooses to give us this gift, in which case we must embrace joy with all our being.

In the face of death, the enjoyment of life is the framing advice of the final section of the book, which can be designated as *ethic*, or, in terms of classical rhetoric, *applicatio* (9:7—12:7). An inner frame, linked to the enjoyment theme, calls to energetic action as long as one has strength. How this is possible is the burden of what is indicated within these frames. In this, naturally, only selected aspects of reality are addressed, those that classical wisdom treated either falsely or not at all: the role of a well-educated person in a political power structure that recruits people on criteria other than objective competence, and stewardship over one's property in an economic system that extends beyond one's horizons, and whose distant center no longer takes care of individuals.

Apart from this ethical section, there is a separate series of admonitions regarding religious behavior. It is like a special supplement that one might name Qoheleth's *religious critique*, inserted in the middle of the social critique (4:17—5:6). In it are criticized some forms of a busy, but frivolous, religiosity. These are contrasted with real "fear of God."

The book as a whole does not present itself as written by Qoheleth. In the frame (1:1-2 and 12:8), and in one place within the book in one of the more difficult passages (7:27), is heard the voice of an otherwise anonymous author, who presents to readers the texts of Qoheleth that then form the contents of the book. This voice—in a synchronic reading—stands out at the end of the book. It formulates two epilogues that defend Qoheleth's often bizarre ideas (at least for many readers), and interpret them in the direction of a legalistic orthodoxy. Historically these were, no doubt, added subsequently, in order to lend the book some support.

History of Interpretation

Yet it seems these ideas did not succeed in persuasion. Many sensitive religious readers have always been uncomfortable with Qoheleth. The very first copyists and translators manipulated parts of the text that wounded their sense of orthodoxy and orthopraxis. Once the Jewish canon was fixed, a discussion about it apparently arose again among the rabbis as to whether Qoheleth belonged among the sacred books. Both Jewish and Christian interpreters alike have long understood very well that in many passages the book meant precisely the opposite of what the literal words said. Samuel ben Meir on the Jewish side and Martin Luther on the Christian side (linked through Nicholas of Lyra) began a new movement to uncover the hidden message of the book. What they began is still not fully completed. And what is one to think when a modern commentator (and he is not alone in this) at the end of his richly empathetic commentary, characterizes the whole negatively, and says that the book provides only a few "rigidified truths," that the Old Testament is "poised to run itself down to death," and that in this degree Qoheleth is its "most startling messianic prophecy" (Hans Wilhelm Hertzberg)? That puts a dialectic in play. It implies further that the canonicity of the book of Qoheleth, and therefore also of the whole Old Testament, is put into question.

Since we began to defend ourselves against the book so early and so mightily, and now, after it has been allowed to show its true face, nevertheless still defend, is it not all the more astonishing that the book previously entered the canon? This leads to questions about its contents, and even more about its historical contexts. Let us begin with the latter, as they may clarify a lot. The book of Qoheleth, at least in the age when it appeared, must have answered many pressing questions and needs of the OT community. Its author must have been someone who was able to win a hearing. There must have been authorities who intervened to achieve the official reception of the book.

Era and Circumstances of Writing

In what time period did Qoheleth originate? Sometimes an early date is proposed on the grounds that parallels are found in very early texts, especially a text from the Old Babylonian Gilgamesh Epic (see the commentary "notes" on 9:7-9). But what we see in these instances are motifs found widely throughout the world, which cannot be used to determine a date. The Epic of Gilgamesh may have been long familiar, in Israel as well as in Mesopotamia. Thus in order to determine a date we must look primarily to the linguistic characteristics and to the problematic situation that the book addresses.

Linguistically, we must date the book as late as possible. Its Hebrew is akin to that of the Mishnah. On the other hand the book of Jesus ben Sirach presupposes the book of Qoheleth. Sirach may be dated between 190 and 180 B.C.E.

The problematic situation of the Maccabean uprising and of the spiritual shift associated with it is not yet mirrored in Qoheleth, but rather the open spirit of world citizenship typical of the Ptolemaic period. During the third century the little temple state of Judea (capital: Jerusalem) belonged, as part of the province "Syria and Phoenicia," to the Ptolemaic Kingdom (capital: Alexandria). It enjoyed far-reaching administrative independence. The Judeans lived according to the ancestral laws of the fathers. Many Jews lived in other parts of Palestine and also in Egypt, especially in Alexandria. Throughout the kingdom, the elite class was Greek, or in the act of adopting Greek culture. There was a Greek military presence and civil administration also in Judea itself. Taxes there were paid in part to the temple (which in turn paid a tribute to the king), and in part directly to the central government. Also the leading families of the elite in Jerusalem were engaged in a process of integration with the leading classes of the kingdom. The decisive symbols of prestige were the Greek language and Greek ways of living. Hellenistic cultural pressure, backed by power, must have been overwhelming at that time. People with a will to learn and capacity to fit in would have been open to it. They adopted its business practices, political rituals, and lifestyle. Above all they learned Greek and had their children educated in Greek. At first this was probably managed through Greek tutors in their homes. But in the third century one can suppose that a private Greek elementary school was already open. It found itself, naturally, in competition with the Hebrew school in the temple. There one learned to read and write on the basis of the book of Proverbs, and then one read the sacred books, especially the Torah. In Greek elementary schools at that time, one first read the whole of Homer, then Hesiod, the lyric poets, and the dramatists (especially Euripides).

The competition between education systems was the visible sign of a much deeper conflict between two whole worldviews. In this conflict the traditional Israelite view was in a difficult situation, and not only because power was no longer on its side. It was caught independently in its own crisis, born of changes in the economic and social relationships in Judea. The ancient "wisdom" of Israel and the fundamental texts of the Torah were formulated in view of a segmented society formed of agricultural small towns and tightly knit communities. Clan and local community were the sources of support and protection. Between individual families the differences in possessions and in social standing were not exaggerated, because the land was equally divided. This had started to change first in the period of the monarchy. At that time the prophets on the one hand, and political catastrophes on the other, slowed this development down. After the return from the exile the same process established itself in Judea once again. In the fifth century Nehemiah introduced a reform, similar in many ways to that of Solon in Athens, that served to prevent the accumulation of properties in the hands of a few, and therefore assured the continued existence of smaller free farmers. In the third century, however, very clearly a process of increasing servitude developed, dispossession, and even slavery for farmers, mostly because of the powerful Alexandrian tax system. This went hand in hand with an incredible enrichment of a small group of leading families and of the high priesthood. Through their participation in the system of contracting tax collection through private individuals, the upper class shared in that governmental concentration of wealth. See the commentary "notes" on 5:7-8. Within this class one could climb very rapidly, but also fall very deeply. In this way the ancient class society inserted itself bit by bit into the society of Judea as well: a cosmopolitan society, driven by capital, administered by the state, stratified, more accessible to individuals but leaving them more rigidly isolated. In it, however, the old philosophy of life, as expressed in the book of Proverbs, for example, was no longer helpful. A lot of what was defined in it was no longer to be found. To follow its shrewd advice could now be singularly unwise. In this situation, the competing Hellenistic mode of thought was not only an opponent, but also at the same time a helping hand. For it had already experienced analogous processes, and it had a very different take on what was now going forward in Judea. Should one not cross over at this point?

A Model of Enculturation

The book of Qoheleth can only be understood as an attempt to profit as much as possible from the Greek understanding of the world, without forcing Israel's wisdom to give up its status. For the old wisdom of Israel (and of the East) is taken for granted within its background of content and of form. On the other hand, its perspective is that of the new reality, as things now stand, fully present, and its inspiration is clearly drawn from Greek education and culture. Let there be no misunderstanding: when we speak nowadays of "Greek education and culture" we usually include, along with Homer, especially names such as Aeschylus and Sophocles among the dramatists, and Plato and Aristotle among the philosophers. At that time, as mentioned above, other authors were read in the schools, authors "more modern" than the great ancient tragedians; and the marketplaces were full especially of popular philosophers: Cynics, Cyrenaics, and Skeptics, along with Epicureans and Stoics. These authors who formed the culture and educational system at that time also provided the ideas and language of the book of Qoheleth, as many factors indicate.

Linguistic Form

Certainly nothing in the book has simply been taken over. It is written consciously, not in the prestige-filled Greek language, but rather in the traditional language of the educated, *Hebrew*. (The street language was Aramaic.) But what kind of Hebrew this is! It is thoroughly new in comparison with the settled and colorful, yet classically simple, language of Proverbs, or with that of the Psalms, the Torah, the historical and prophetic books. Here attention has been paid to the way this Aramaic-speaking people actually talked. A writer has worked out philosophical concepts in the language of merchants. Greek syntax and stereotypes of speech in Greek culture mark the Hebrew just as today in central Europe elements of English are heard in the technical jargon of many intellectuals. But thereby the language touches reality more closely, and in this new medium the way is opened for new literary forms to evolve. A fundamental new form is the *poikilometron*, which is born of Semitic roots but was then developed by the Cynic Menippos of Gadara. It consists of a mixture of prose with verses written in diverse meters. This includes above all a philosophical prose unknown in Israel before this book: observations marshaled in a row, a line of thought developing step for step, motifs dropped and then picked up again, commenting on venerable sayings by cleverly reformulating them so that they mimic the old but affirm something new. It also includes a new kind of poetry to which the language of prose can effortlessly rise. This functions in such a way that the classical poetic figures of speech such as parallelism, assonance and rhyme, linkword chiasm, and strophic form serve as elements of a lower order that generate expectations of classical form and content, not in order to fulfill them, but rather so that the final statement might be constructed precisely in opposition to them. The whole book is laced together by an artful use of key words, in a manner that is not otherwise to be found in the ancient Near East. There results a mysterious web in which every element is connected with all the others, and all interpreters who attempt to find a single linear line of thought become helplessly tangled in this subtler universe of discourse. Yet there is an organization to the whole. Most certainly it does not consist of an accumulation of "sayings" set out in a series by someone else.

Structure

On the one hand, one is drawn to recognize in it those principles of composition that were worked out at that time by the Cynics into the form of philosophical diatribe, with their exploitation of language resources for purposes of effect and of persuasion. The survey of contents given above reveals an explicit content dynamic. Early on, after a few attention-grabbing units, the central thesis is clearly stated. Then it is deepened, defended, and worked out in daily applications.

1:2-11	Opening (theses, questions, underlying cosmology)
1:12—3:15	Narrative introduction to the primarily anthropological central thesis
3:16—6:10	Deepening through many glimpses of social experience
6:11—9:6	*Refutatio* of contrary positions, especially of older wisdom
9:7—12:8	*Applicatio* through concrete proposals about human behavior

On the other hand, there is also retained the art of chiastically structured previews, and especially the principle of symmetric ordering of the textual materials, inherited from Semitic rhetorical practice and its care for balance. Let us clarify this too in connection with the survey of contents given above. The organization of the text, as most convincingly perceived in its logic and rhetoric, satisfies a Greek sensibility. Yet the "religious critique," when judged by that premise, is located out of proper order. Indeed, it functions, for Semitic sensibility, as the center of a palistrophic structure that also informs the text as a whole. This can be shown as follows:

1:2-3	Frame
1:4-11	Cosmology (poem)
1:12—3:15	Anthropology
3:16—4:16	Social critique I
4:17—5:6	Religious critique
5:7—6:10	Social critique II
6:11—9:6	Deconstruction
9:7—12:7	Ethic (concludes with a poem)
12:8	Frame

We see here an almost playfully worked out interweaving of diatribe and palistrophe. It reveals a supreme art in the use of literary form, and also a settled refusal, amid total openness to Greek, to give up one's own heritage. What is true of form is equally true of message.

The Israelite Content

As one reads this book, however present one often seems to be to the world of those poets who feel life is essentially ephemeral, or to the world of one of the Cyrenaics, or Empiricists, or Skeptics, one possibly exiled from his Greek city-state because of his atheism, or however remote from Hebrew thought may appear the book's beginning with the image of an eternal and gloriously revolving cosmos—at the same time, equally present is the theocentric premise of the book: God's sovereignty and his participation in determining all human events, a participation conceived more radically than in previous Israelite wisdom writings, and equally taken for granted is the presentation of "a king over Israel in Jerusalem" as the chosen example of human success and good fortune. The Book of Job had to affirm the validity for all humankind of Israel's wisdom, and to this end named a non-Israelite as its hero. In Qoheleth the reverse process is underway, and so those modern interpreters who name Qoheleth's God a "Fate," a "despot," or a "Creator God" have completely misunderstood the real context of the book. What is new, and also required, needs to be assimilated, but in such a way that it not be necessary to send the children to a Greek school; in such a way also that future generations will continue to come to the temple, not so much in order to offer sacrifice (the heathen also do this), but rather to listen when there are readings from the Torah and the Prophets, and to grow in the *fear of God*. That message is to be read in the center of the book. It reveals its purpose.

Whether it succeeded is another question. In fact the hellenizing influence continued to grow among the elite families. In the end it triggered the Maccabean revolts as a reaction. Jewish identity was ultimately preserved through military power and national segregation, for a time at least, and not through this earlier attempt at cultural control. We do not know what influence the book of Qoheleth had in its early years. Had it, contrary to its intentions, actually strengthened the hellenizing process, simply because it had not condemned it? Or had it indeed shown a way for many to be modern and realistic, without having to abandon their own identity? We will never be able to find that out. Here we have been concerned primarily with the insight that the book of Qoheleth was an attempt to achieve something that Jewish thinkers in third-century Israel had to consider as of supreme importance. There were expectations from this undertaking. Naturally there was needed a star-quality writer who could carry it off.

Authorship

Since the book Qoheleth does not present itself as a book written by a man named "Qoheleth," but rather presents his sayings, one is drawn to ask whether this is even an historical person. "Qoheleth" could represent the ideal philosopher. The narratives about him in the first "postscript" could indeed be fictional. On the other hand, it seems that the book's author did not write this first postscript. So it may well be that it is based on facts, and there was a "Qoheleth." But "Qoheleth" could hardly have been his real name. That was more likely a pseudonym or nickname. There were such names at that time. For example, in Alexandria the Cyrenaic Hegesias was named Peisithanatos, that is, "suicide advisor." The most probable meaning of "Qoheleth" is "assembler" or "leader of the assembly." But leader of which assembly? Nothing in the book suggests the national (political) assembly, which possibly met from time to time in those years, and which could have been named *qāhāl*. Still less does it suggest the cultic community, which could also have carried that name. The Greek word that corresponds to Hebrew *qāhāl* is *ekklēsia*. Sometimes it signifies a philosophical circle. Similarly *ekklēsiastēs* = *qōhelet* could have been the nickname of the founder and leader of such a group.

At that time, books like Qoheleth did not normally get written as purely literary works, but rather in connection with a teaching or educational responsibility. On the other hand, the content and form of Qoheleth are of such a character that one could hardly imagine their origin to lie in the very familiar framework of temple schooling, a centuries-old institution with fixed practices and materials. Those addressed in it do not even carry the title, traditional there, of "my son." There is no indication of any special consideration that the students might have priestly activities in the future, or professional dealings with the Torah. Moreover, the evaluation of earlier educational tradition, as it is seen in the "deconstruction" section, is quite frank. This leads inevitably out to the more obscure periphery of the official cultural establishment, on the margin of the traditional school system. In the first postscript of the book we read that Qoheleth had not only become a *ḥākām*, but moreover had brought information to the *'am*, the "people" (12:9). *Ḥākām* can mean simply "educated," "learned," but it can also denote the teacher of a school. Was Qoheleth originally, or still, a teacher in the temple school? But then what did he do "moreover"? Perhaps he had in some way opened the door to culture for new groups from the lower classes. This later became an item in the program of the Pharisaic party. But perhaps we are here dragging a second- and first-century problematic back into the third century. It is more likely, in our context, that Qoheleth offered his teaching publicly in the marketplace, as did the Greek peripatetic philosophers. Now that must have been something new in Jerusalem, and it would have excited a lot of attention. A group of students gathered around him, and from this he acquired the name "Qoheleth." Either he, or his editor, flirted with this allusion in the book that later gathered his teaching together.

Anyone who managed to do this in Jerusalem must have been not only a (probably well-traveled) person of broad culture with high spiritual and linguistic abilities, but also a powerful personality, able to get things done. A lot becomes easier to understand if we presume that he came from a powerful family. This would make him one of those who could not easily be forbidden to take chances. Moreover, if the tentative hypothesis that follows below is correct, concerning the surprising (to say the least) process of acceptance of this book into the canon, then he must even have come from one of the priestly families who had a say in the temple school, because authoritative people from that milieu must later at some point have stood up for him.

The Book and the Canon

We can form only conjectures about the process of acceptance of the book into the canon. The most fruitful starting point will be to reflect that when, a century or so after Qoheleth, the idea arose of establishing a canon of sacred scriptures, it was probably not a question of collecting "inspired" texts as a later generation conceived it to be, even though "inspiration" was part of the picture in prophetic texts (and both Moses and David were counted as prophets). They were probably simply drawing up an acquisitions list for good synagogue libraries. To do this they did not evaluate individual books according to abstract criteria, such as orthodoxy, or the reputation of their authors, or being written before a determined date. Rather they simply accepted the books that were already in use for the activities carried on in the temple and in well-established synagogues. These activities were not restricted to worship or law courts, but they also included school education. Thus the schoolbooks that were used in the temple school in Jerusalem, and also in the comparable synagogue schools, automatically ended up in the canon. The book of Qoheleth must have been among them at that time. Therefore, the real question is, How did Qoheleth get to be a schoolbook in Jerusalem?

One might easily surmise that soon after Qoheleth's time the pressure increased on the temple school to modernize, that is, to be open to Greek education. The founding of a Greek elementary school and the threat of also soon opening a Greek *gymnasion* (which actually happened in 175 B.C.E. and which triggered the Maccabean revolt) must have drawn students away and caused fears of ever increasing defections. Parents may well have given ultimatums. In such situations there is only one solution: give in to demands, many of which are justified, but in such a way that you do not give up your own identity. A compromise could be reached: the introduction of an existing book, Qoheleth, as a school text-book. Qoheleth was "modern," but it was written by a man from among their own ranks, and in Hebrew. The debate among the faculty about making this a textbook may have made its mark in the book itself. The former school textbooks—Proverbs with its various collections, and pos-sibly the Song of Songs—came from Solomon or other wise kings of old. For this reason a title was added at the beginning that served more or less well to make the new textbook also into a Solomonic book. Moreover, the first postscript was added. It merely underlines the importance of Qoheleth and explicitly makes clear that the book was to be considered one of the wisdom collections. Within the context of its time it meant that the book was recognized as a school textbook. Most likely Proverbs con-tinued to be used as a first-level text, and then Qoheleth for higher grades.

The book of Sirach was composed soon after. It may have been an attempt to bring a radical and completely new perspective to the textbook system, which had proved unsatisfactory even after Qoheleth was included. But it already reflected a whole new phase of development, for it not only intended to replace Proverbs and Qoheleth in one stroke, but it also linked the normative culture of Israel directly to the Law and the Prophets to a degree that until now had been unheard of. Thus was opened the path, right in the intellectual center of Jerusalem, to the new interpretation of their own religious tradition, which went consciously against the hell-enizing influences. One important figure in this movement may well have been Simeon, son of Jochanan, who receives an extraordinary measure of praise at the end of Sirach. The plan for a curricular reform so radical that all earlier textbooks were to be replaced needed approval at the highest level. It is not certain that Sirach was ever, in fact, adopted as a school-book. Certainly, Proverbs and Qoheleth were not discontinued. External events must have intervened. Jason, the second son of Simeon, became an exponent of the radical Hellenistic party. Then the whole family ended up in the whirlpool of events that led to the Maccabean revolt, and it lost its position. The view that the book of Sirach took regarding this widely hated family now stood in its way.

Whatever the details of this story, the second postscript of Qoheleth may well have come from the time of debate whether to create a new school text. It seems to try to arouse even the students (addressed as "my son") against the plan to prepare new textbooks, since these would only increase their burden of class materials. At the same time it defended the orthodoxy of the book, which no doubt the protagonists of a more tradition-oriented curriculum reform had questioned, by attributing back to Qoheleth the proposed leading theme of Sirach's new textbook: "Fear God, and keep his commandments." At the same time, another addition was inserted in 11:9 in order to protect Qoheleth from criticism at its most sensitive place.

Literary Genre

If the reader perceives this book as belonging to these (or very similar) historical circumstances, then many apparent obstacles are resolved, especially questions about those items that are usually thought to be missing in it. It is a book in the ambit of education, and, more precisely, of adult reeducation. It is written for those who, it takes for granted, hear the Law and the Prophets read in the temple, and who have also learned the older wisdom. Otherwise, it could not so clearly play upon the opening chapters of Genesis, adopt proposals from Deuteronomy, and skip over so much that is well expressed, as is, in Proverbs. It may have known of other attempts to mediate entry to the Greek world, and have left a lot up to them. For example, reflection in narrative form about the possibility of living as a believing Jew in the highest circles of a world kingdom, structurally anti-God, which currently the author of the Daniel legends was presenting. Or the apologetic-missionary transmission of the biblical protohistory and of the story of Abraham, addressed to the Greek intellectual world, which was undertaken at the same time by an anonymous Samaritan, in Greek language of course. Eusebius preserved some fragments of it but gave him the erroneous name Eupolemos. Moreover, Qoheleth was not intended for everybody, but rather for a determined age group from a specific social class. It recommends actions that correspond to the special location of this group within a general situation that they, from their place in Jerusalem, could hardly have influenced. It recognizes that God wants justice for humankind; it calls the evil of its world by name, without fear; it is driven by hunger for justice and well-being; but it does not propose a revolutionary utopia. Rather it suggests some political-economical options and otherwise tries only to show how individuals might take some reasonable steps. It is the book of a teacher and thinker, not of a prophet or guerrilla warrior.

It proceeds, moreover, with extraordinary caution. It is only within a framework narrative that Qoheleth himself is heard to speak, and this literary form establishes a distancing from his words that would not otherwise be possible. The actual author of the book makes no assertions of his own. He merely reports what another has thought and said. Even this other does not simply lay out his opinions. He again tells stories. He tells of his experiences, and shows how, through them, he came to see things in certain ways. Often he offers only questions. At great length he even pretends to be someone else, namely the famous King Solomon. All of these devices are literary techniques that free the readers to think their own thought and come to their own conclusions.

Qoheleth's Philosophy

There is an even more far-reaching relativity of affirmation. It resides in the special "philosophy" of the book. In respect to modern thought, this philosophy is surprisingly similar to existentialism. The social context within which existentialism arose was certainly comparable: in Europe the breakdown in the divisions of a society mainly structured by lineages, which was ever increasingly evident during the approach to, and first half of, the twentieth century; the horizontal growth of class solidarity; increasing isolation and rootlessness of individuals in an ever more technical and international society. It happened, moreover, among the middle and upper classes rather than among the poor. Qoheleth could have encountered other Greek philosophical schools as well. If precisely the "popular philosophy" spoke so strongly to him, that may not be due only to the fact that it had the loudest voice in the intellectual marketplace, but also that its voice was most in keeping with Israel's experience of individual helplessness due to social change, in a world that no longer seemed intelligible.

Now, just as the leading modern existential philosophers were not merely a voice for an existential mood swing in European culture, but also produced written works whose analyses remain, and are either true or false, so also is Qoheleth to be scrutinized, in what he has left behind, concerning any insight that may be judged either true or false. It could be the case that a specific cultural mood was required before insights such as his could break through. Once they have been achieved, however, they stand on their own. The book of Qoheleth is the *most transparent place, within the Bible, where Israel meets with Greek philosophy*. It establishes primarily for theologians the requirement, rooted right in the canon of Scripture—and this cuts across the division between the two Testaments—that they carry out the hard philosophical work of systematic clarification in respect to every Christian discourse.

Let me explain this further. Qoheleth analyzes human existence as being in the time that is given only in the now that accompanies human living and that (for individuals) ends at death. It can be experienced as happiness. It is more than a falling into nothingness, because in its individually specific form it originates in the eternity of God, who transcends this world and yet is always at work in each event. His action is perfect. Even evil he sets aright. But humans cannot see through the activity of God, and so they find it inexplicable and amoral. We know, of course, that there is a meaning to it all, but we have no grasp of it—only God has that. We can rely only on whatever, in each moment, comes to us from the hand of God.

The Theological Challenge of Qoheleth

If this is true, there then arise some far-reaching hermeneutical problems for the customary ways in which the Bible talks about God and his activity in the world, especially for language dealing with what is usually termed "sacred history." Now it would be wrong simply to stop speaking, because of Qoheleth, about God's participation in history, of the choosing of a people, of personal relationship with God, of the communicability of God's will, and a promised future. But such speaking must understand itself in such a way as not to fall behind the radical *God-world metaphysics* of Qoheleth and return to myth. Wherever this speaking becomes theologically explicit, it must be possible to give a clear and systematic account of it. The great theologians have always seen this as part of their task, whether they worked from Greek systems of thought or from modern philosophy. It has become fashionable among exegetes, when comparing Qoheleth to the rest of the Bible, to label him with phrases such as "no personal God," "denial of human freedom," "abandoning the idea of sacred history," "loss of trust in living." But this is no more than a flight from the demand that the book makes for theological thinking. It also runs the risk of falsely understanding the very thing that one had intended to defend.

Related to the radical teaching of the book about God-and-world was also its *radical focus on this-worldliness*. Qoheleth has this in common with almost the whole Old Testament. There were veiled and hidden corrections within its this-worldliness, especially in the image of the underworld as a place of shadowy afterlife that could be improved through the mindfulness of the living and sacrifices offered for the dead. From the Greek world a notion of immortality in the Platonic tradition was introduced, with its devaluation of all material reality. Apocalyptic expectations, which arose at that time and were directly addressed by

Introduction

Qoheleth, could be just as effective in questioning the seriousness of death as end, if their world imagery was taken to be real. In opposition to this, Qoheleth sharply emphasized the terminal nature of death, and in this he was also following the popular philosophy. The last books of the Old Testament, and the New Testament, fully legitimate Christian speaking about the other world. However, this should not be used simply to declare Qoheleth wrong. Death does remain the total end of a human being insofar as he or she lives in the time that accompanies living. Christian hope regarding afterlife must be such that it does not cover over the terminal character of death and the continued dependence of all human things on this life. Medieval theology secured this by its distinction between *status viae* and *status termini*. This expressed the fact that one's earthly time, with its ever open possibilities for each next moment, is completely cut off through death. That other life, which one hoped to find in God, can be understood only as fruit, or summing up and final fulfillment, of the fleeting time on earth. If we want to formulate this in the perspective of Qoheleth's thought, it cannot be done by declaring his notions of death as end to be false, but rather by thinking through and deepening the implications of his affirmations that every human activity is equally God's activity, that God's activity is perfect, that every event includes eternity. In this regard Qoheleth had merely inserted an ancient mythical convention, and to this he only alludes: the *eternal return* of all things. This image of an eternal cycle structuring the cosmos is not, as almost all commentators suggest, an image of despair, but rather it is completely positive. It means the participation of beings in continuous Being. These images of the cosmos, which modern science has left far behind but which here control the imagination, make it difficult for us to enter this area of his thought. Yet we must not lose sight of it when he is talking about his dialectic of death and life. In any case, here death does not lose its seriousness. Each present moment is given unending value, a value that, however, can be conceived only through trust in the God who surpasses our conceiving. No "other world" can be used to legitimate a flight from the responsibility of this moment, and to console.

Thus Qoheleth is a critical case against the dangers hidden in the Christian message. There is more. There will be enduring meaning for his most characteristic project: his destruction of any ultimate equation that could claim to give humans control over the future, along with his invitation to place oneself in the openness of each next moment, simply in God's hands. Very often, the analogous translation for our time is easy to find. Here we must note, above all, that one can point out many similarities to Jesus of Nazareth, who came as a peripatetic preacher. He too, through many parables, called into question the plausibility of his interlocutors. Did Jesus' householder (= God) act according to moralistic expectations when he paid those who had worked one hour in the vineyard precisely as much as those who had born the heat of the day? The midrash to Qoheleth contains a parallel parable that ends up precisely opposed to this parable of Jesus, since it provides the moral justification for the householder's action. Thus both Qoheleth and Jesus stand corrected. Now the God of Jesus, like the God of Qoheleth, has his sun rise not only over the good but also over the wicked. The kingship of God announced by Jesus makes the world just as unintelligible and places humans in the ever new astonishing moment, just as does the word of Qoheleth. And in it, just as for Qoheleth, one cannot always obey the law: Jesus' fear of God causes him to break the divine commandment concerning the Sabbath. These analogies between Jesus and Qoheleth, which could be multiplied, have hardly been noted before now.

If we reflect on the points that are analogous, we also find a difference in each one. Qoheleth remains the *teacher* who uncovers and shows. When he has finished speaking, he has to allow his students to go on being influenced, and they must seek their way from moment to moment in a society that they now see as corrupt. If they go to the temple or to the synagogues, there they will hear the Torah of Moses and the word of the Prophets, which declare God's will for society and demand that it be carried out. The priests do not live according to their words, however, and no one else can be found who could really bring about the kingship of God. Jesus uncovers and shows, just as Qoheleth did; but then he also refers to himself, and can say that we should *follow him*. In this he, and he alone, creates the possibility of letting go the assurances of the old society of this world and of truly living each moment in the kingship of God. Qoheleth still had to say that even the just man did not know whether God loved or despised him. Those who follow Jesus know that they are loved, even if they are sinners. It is only in this context that one may say about Qoheleth that he belongs to the Old Testament.

Translation

1:1 The words of Qoheleth, the son of David, who was king in
Jerusalem.

  2 "A breath, a puff of breath .,. . a breath, a puff of breath," Qoheleth
used to say, "they all are a breath." 3 What profit does one draw
from all the possessions for which one labors under the sun?

      4 A generation passes, another comes,
        the earth stays in eternity.

      5 The sun, which rose and then set,
        breathless it races back to the place where it rises again.

      6 Southward blowing, and turning to the north,
        turning, turning, blows the air,
        and because it turns, the air returns.

      7 All the streams flow to the sea;
        the sea does not fill—
        to the place whence the streams flow
        there they return to flow again.

      8 All things are constantly restless,
        more than humans can express:
        the eye is not sated by observing;
        the ear is not filled by hearing.

      9 Whatever has occurred, that will occur again.
        What has been carried out, that will be carried out again.
        There is nothing new under the sun.

     10 At times something happens about which they say:
        "Observe that—that is new"—
        but it has already occurred in the eternities
        that have gone before us.

     11 There is no memory of the former ones;
        and of the future ones, still to come,
        there will also be no memory of them
        among those who will come after them.

  12 I am Qoheleth. I was king over Israel in Jerusalem. 13 I had
made up my mind to examine and to explore, with the help of

knowledge, whether all that is carried out under the heavens is really a bad business in which humankind is forced to be involved, at a god's command. 14 I observed all the actions that are carried out under the sun. The conclusion: all are a breath, an inspiration of air.

> 15 What is bent cannot be straightened;
> what is not there cannot be counted.

16 I thought to myself as follows. Look: I have increased and expanded my knowledge, so that now I have surpassed everyone who has ruled over Jerusalem before me. I have often been able to observe knowledge and perception. 17 So I took upon myself to perceive what knowledge really is, and to perceive what delusion and ignorance really are. I perceived that this also is a spirit of air. 18 For

> Much knowledge—much vexation;
> deeper perception—deeper pain.

2:1 I said to myself, Go ahead, try being joyful, taste happiness. The conclusion: that too is a breath.

> 2 About laughter I said: What nonsense!
> About joy: What good is it?

3 I drove myself to exploration in order to bathe my body in wine. And my mind kept leading my knowledge to pasture in order to imprison ignorance until I might observe what kind of happiness humans can bring about under the heavens during the few days of their lives. 4 I expanded my action:

> I built houses for myself;
> I planted vineyards for myself.
> 5 I set out gardens and parks for myself;
> in them I planted all sorts of trees.
> 6 I arranged overflowing ponds,
> so as to water the stands of sprouting trees.
> 7 I bought male and female slaves,
> although I already owned house slaves.
> I owned also a large number of animals, cattle, sheep, and
>   goats,
> more than all those who preceded me in Jerusalem.
> 8 I collected silver and gold for myself as well
> and, as my personal possession, kings and provinces.
> I procured singers, male and female, trained for me,
> and what a man desires: a large harem.

9 I was already great, and I increased even more, so that I surpassed all those who preceded me in Jerusalem. Moreover, my knowledge remained with me, 10 and whatever my eyes desired I

did not withhold from them. I did not have to deny my heart any joy. For my heart could draw joy from all my possessions. And that was my portion out of all my possessions.

11 And I reflected on all the actions that my hands had carried out, and on the possessions that I had labored to possess. The conclusion: they are all a breath and an inspiration of air. There is no profit under the sun.

12 I reflected, by observing what knowledge and what delusion and ignorance really are. Moreover, what kind of human will succeed the king whom they had earlier established? 13 I observed: yes, a profit comes from knowledge, and not from ignorance, just as there is a profit from light rather than from darkness:

> 14 One who knows has eyes in his head;
> a fool walks in darkness.

But I perceived: Me too! For one and the same fate awaits each one. 15 So I thought to myself: the fate that awaits the fool also awaits me. Why then have I gathered knowledge beyond measure? And I said to myself that this too is a breath. 16 For there is no eternal memory of a person who knows, any more than of a fool, for in the days just ahead both will be forgotten. How can it be that the one who knows must die just like the fool? 17 And living became irksome to me, for the actions that are carried out under the sun weighed on me as an evil. Yes, all are a breath and an inspiration of air.

18 And also irksome to me were all my possessions for which I am laboring under the sun, and which I must leave behind for some human who will come after me. 19 Who perceives whether it will be one who knows or one who does not know? And yet someone will have power over all my possessions for which I have labored under the sun, and applied my knowledge. This too is a breath.

20 And then I turned to despair concerning all my possessions, for which I am laboring under the sun. 21 For it happens that the possessions which one person has accumulated through knowledge and perception and skill must be handed over as the portion of another person who has not labored for it. This too is a breath and a recurring evil.

22 What then does a person get out of all one's possessions and by weaving plans in one's mind, in all one's labor under the sun?

> 23 Day after day business consists only of pains and vexation;
> and even at night one's mind is not at rest.

That too is a breath.

24 That happy disposition, whereby one can eat and drink and come to perceive happiness in one's possessions, is not a given in

human nature. My observation has been rather that this comes from the hand of God. 25 For who, if not I, has something to eat, or is able to enjoy? 26 Now there are humans who are blessed in the eyes of God. They are the ones to whom he has given knowledge, and perception, and joy. And there are those whose life has failed. They are the ones whom he has commanded to be involved in the business of increasing and collecting, and then of giving it all to the one who is blessed in the eyes of God. That too is a breath and an inspiration of air.

3:1 Everything has its hour. For every interest under the heavens there is an appointed time:

  2 A time to give birth
  and a time to die;
  a time to plant,
  and a time to harvest the plants;

  3 a time to kill
  and a time to heal;
  a time to tear down
  and a time to build;

  4 a time to cry
  and a time to laugh;
  a time of lament
  and a time of dance;

  5 a time to throw stones
  and a time to gather stones;
  a time to embrace
  and a time to stay arm's length;

  6 a time to search
  and a time to give up for lost;
  a time to keep
  and a time to throw away;

  7 a time to tear
  and a time to sew;
  a time to be silent
  and a time to speak;

  8 a time to love
  and a time to hate;
  a time of war
  and a time of peace.

9 When anyone takes action, what profit does he make from his labor? 10 I had now observed the business in which humans are forced to be involved because of a god's command. 11 All that, he has enacted perfectly in its time. Moreover he has put eternity in

all of it, but not in such a way that humans could find out the action which God has carried out from its beginning to its end. 12 I perceived that in all of it there is no happiness in activities, except in so far as one can be joyful and in this way enact happiness during one's own lifetime. 13 And, what is more: when a person is able to eat and drink and taste happiness in all his possessions, that is always a gift of God. 14 And I perceived that every action that God carries out occurs in eternity. To it nothing can be added and nothing taken away, and God has made humans fear him.

15 Whatever is occurring now, has already been there;
and whatever is to be, has already occurred;
and God will search for whatever has been chased off.

16 There is something else that I have observed under the sun:
in the very place of justice, there is lawlessness;
and in the very place of law-abiding, there is lawlessness.

17 So I thought to myself: it is God who judges both the law-abiding and the lawless. For

for every interest there is an appointed time,
and for every action in that place.

18 With regard to humans as individuals, I thought to myself, God has singled them out and (from this) they must recognize that in reality they are animals. 19 For

fate awaits each human,
and fate awaits the animals.
One single fate awaits both.

As these die, so the others die. Both share the same air. There is in this no advantage for the human over the animal. Both are a breath. 20 They both pass to one place.

They both come alive out of the dust;
and both return to the dust.

21 Who perceives if the air of a human really goes upward, while the air of an animal descends down to earth?

22 So I have observed that there is no happiness except in so far as one finds joy in one's activity. That is one's portion. Who could enable a person to taste something that will happen only afterward?

4:1 Again, I further observed all that is carried out under the sun in order to exploit people. Just look:

the exploited ones weep,
and no one comforts them;
from the hands of those who exploit them comes violence,
and no one comforts them.

2 I always congratulate the dead who have already died, and not the living who must still go on living. 3 I would consider to be still happier than either the one who has not been as yet, and who has not observed the evil activity that is carried on under the sun.

4 And I observed that every labor and every successful action means rivalry between people. That too is breath and an inspiration of air.

> 5 The fool folds his hands,
> and eats his own flesh.
> 6 Better a handful with quiet
> than two handfuls with labor and an inspiration of air.

7 Again, I further observed a breath under the sun. 8 It happens that a person stands alone, and there is no second. Yes, not even a son or brother. But his possessions are limitless, and moreover his eyes are not sated by wealth. But for whom am I laboring, and why deny myself happiness? That too is a breath; it is a bad business. 9 Two are better than one, if it happens they are well rewarded by their possessions. 10 For if they fall, the one can lift up his partner. Too bad for the one who falls, with no second to help him up. 11 Moreover:

> When two sleep together, they warm one another;
> but how will one alone get warm?
> 12 And if someone can overpower one person,
> still two will resist him;
> and a three-ply cord
> will not soon be broken.
> 13 Better a poor young man who knows,
> than a king who is old but a fool—

because he no longer perceived that he should take advice. 14 The young man was freed from prison and became king, even though he had come into the world destitute, while the other already reigned. 15 But I observed that all the living who walked about under the sun sided with the next young man who arose in his place. 16 The people carry on, whoever it is that leads them. Moreover, the most recent generation will not be full of joy about him either. For that too is a breath and a spirit of air.

> 17 Watch your step
> when you go to the house of God.
> Enter in order to listen,
> and not, as the fools do, in order to deliver a sacrifice.
> They do not even perceive
> how to do evil.
> 5:1 Don't be too fast with your mouth;
> and in your heart don't burn

to make a speech in the presence of God.

2 God is in heaven,
you are on the earth,
so let your words be few.
Dreams come with a multiplicity of business;
and the voice of a fool with a multiplicity of words.

3 When you make a vow to God,
don't delay in carrying it out.
God takes no interest in a fool:
Whatever you vow, carry it out.

4 It is better to vow nothing,
than to vow and not carry it out.

5 Don't permit your mouth
to bring your flesh down into sin.
Never declare before the messenger:
"It was an oversight."
Why should God rage about what you are saying,
and destroy the actions of your hands?

6 Rather, when dreams multiply, and puffs of breath and
endless words,
then fear God.

7 When you observe that the poor in the province are destitute, and justice and law-abiding thwarted, don't be surprised when interests work this way:
one higher up covers for another,
and others even higher up are behind both of them.

8 But still it profits the land when a king takes care of its fields.

9 One who loves money
never has his fill of money;
and anyone who loves luxuries
never has sufficient income—that too is a breath.

10 When prosperity increases,
the numbers of those who eat it increase.
What benefit remains for the owner?
His eyes can only look.

11 Sweet is the sleep of the worker,
whether he has a little to eat or a lot.
The full belly of the wealthy man
does not let him rest in sleep.

12 Something evil happens, something like a disease, that I have observed under the sun: gathered wealth, placed for its owner in the bank, is lost in bankruptcy. 13 Through bad business dealings, this wealth was lost. The owner had fathered a son, but now there is nothing in his accounts. 14 As he came from his mother's

womb—naked, as he came, so must he once again begin his life. There is nothing which he can ever draw from his possessions, which he had deposited in his account. 15 So this too is something evil, something like a disease. Just as he once came, so must he begin his life again. And what profit does he gain laboring for air? 16 Even more:

> All of his days he will eat in darkness,
> with constant vexation, and illness and depression.

17 Consider what I have observed—perfect happiness consists in this: to eat and drink and taste happiness through all one's possessions for which one has labored under the sun during the few days of life that God has given one. For that is one's portion. 18 Moreover, always, when God has given a person wealth and holdings, and has empowered one to consume them and maintain one's portion and find joy in one's possessions, the real divine gift consists in this, 19 that one will not much remember how few are the days of one's life, because God continuously answers through the joy in one's heart.

6:1 There happens one evil which I have observed under the sun, and it weighs heavily on individuals. 2 God gives someone so much wealth, holdings, and honor that he lacks nothing of whatever his gullet desires, but God does not empower him to eat it, because a stranger eats it. That is a breath and it is an evil disease.

3 If someone has a hundred children and lives many years, so that his life is really long, and if his prosperity cannot serve to sate his gullet, even if no grave were awaiting him, I say: a stillborn child is better than that person. 4 Because:

> As a breath it came,
> into darkness it passes,
> in darkness its name remains covered.

5 Moreover, it has never observed or perceived the sun. So it is at rest, whereas he is not. 6 And if he lives two thousand years, but does not taste happiness, do not both pass to one and the same place? 7 All human labor is for the jaws of death, and its gullet is never satisfied. 8 What profit for the one who knows over the fool; or what for the poor, however perceptive, in making his way among the living?

> 9 Better to have something before your eyes
> than to have a hungry gullet.
> That too is a breath and an inspiration of air.

> 10 Whatever has occurred
> it was already called by name.
> It was also perceived

that each one is only human,
and that he cannot fight
with someone stronger than himself.

11 There happen many words that only multiply breath. Of what profit
are they to a person? 12 For who perceives what is better for a
person in their lifetime, during the few living days of one's breath,
which one carries out like a shadow? And who can tell anyone
what will occur afterward under the sun?

7:1 Better a name esteemed than scented creams—
   and the day one dies than the day one was born;

2 better go to a hall of grieving
   than go to a festive hall.
   Since this is the end of all humans,
   let those who still live lay it to heart.

3 Better vexation than laughter,
   for by a troubled face are hearts headed aright.

4 The heart of those who know is in a hall of grieving,
   the heart of fools in a hall of joy.

5 It is better to listen to the criticism of one who knows,
   than to become fans of the song of fools.

6 For, like the crackling of thorns under the pot,
   so is the laughter of a fool.—

But that too is a breath, because:

7 Blackmail dulls the wit of the wise
   and a bribe leads understanding astray.

8 Better the outcome of anything than its beginning;
   better an air of caution than an air of impatience.

9 Don't be blown about in an air of your vexation;
   For vexation is at home in the belly of fools.—

10 Do not ask:
   How came it about that earlier times
   were better than present times?

For such a question will not make you appear knowledgeable.

11 Knowledge is as good as an inheritance,
   and is even more profitable for those who see the sun;

12 for one who shelters in the shadow of knowledge,
   is also in the shadow of money;
   but the profit from perception is
   that knowledge keeps its owner alive.—

13 But note the actions of God: for:
Who can make straight what he has bent?

14 On a happy day, take part in the happiness; and on a bad day,
take note: God has made the latter just as he made the former, so

that humans can find out nothing about what comes afterward.
15 In my days of breath I have observed both cases: it happens
that a law-abiding person, despite the law-abiding, comes to a bad
end; it happens that a lawless person, despite the lawlessness,
has a long life. 16 Don't be altogether too law-abiding and don't
profit too much from what you know: why should you destroy yourself? 17 Don't be utterly lawless, or become totally ignorant: why
should you die before it is time? 18 It is best you hold on to the
one without losing your grip on the other. A God-fearer, in any
case, will escape both dangers.

> 19 For one who knows, knowledge is a protection more
>   powerful
> than the ten rulers
> who have dominated the city.—

20 And yet there has never been a human on earth who was so law-
abiding that he did what was right, without ever sinning. 21 And
don't listen to everything people say. For you will never hear someone under you speak critically of you, 22 and yet you clearly perceive that you have often spoken critically of others.
23 In all ways I tried having knowledge. I said: I will study to become
learned. But knowledge remained distant for me.

> 24 Distant whatever has occurred,
> and deep in the depths—
> who could ever find it?

25 So I turned, that is, my mind turned me, around. I wanted to perceive through exploration and search out what that knowledge is
which is reckoned from specific observations. Moreover, I wanted
to perceive whether lawlessness was connected with a lack of
learning and ignorance with delusion. 26 Again and again I find
the claim that womankind is stronger than death. Because:

> She is a ring of siege towers,
> and her heart a net,
> her arms are ropes.
> One blessed in the eyes of God can escape from her;
> one whose life has failed is taken by her.

27 But look at what, in observation after observation, I have found
out, said Qoheleth, until I eventually found the final reckoning;
28 or, more precisely, how I constantly searched and found
nothing:

> Among a thousand I could find one human only;
> but the one I found, among them all, was not a woman.

29 Look at the one thing I found out:

> God made human beings straightforward,

but they have gone searching for all sorts of reckonings.

8:1 Who then is the one who knows? Who perceives the sense of a proverb?

> The knowledge of a man makes his face radiant,
> and his stony features soften.—

2 But I (to the contrary): Be attentive to the orders of the king, because of the oath you swore before a god. 3 Do not withdraw hastily from his presence, and do not insist on something if it threatens to have an evil ending. For whatever he finds interesting he will carry out. 4 Since behind the word of the king there is power, who can ask him: What are you doing?

> 5 One attentive to the law will have no occasion to perceive evil,
> a knowing mind perceives when the time is right.—

6 Nevertheless:

> There happens a right time for every interest,

and:

> Human evil is often heavy upon a person.

and:

> 7 One does not perceive what will occur,

and:

> How it will occur, who will tell that?
> 8 There is no human who has power over the air,
> so that he might lock up the air.
> There is no power over the day of death.
> There is no day off in a war.
> Even a crime will not win freedom for the criminal.

9 I observed all of this while I was examining all the actions that were being carried out under the sun, during a period when one man was using power over another in order to bring evil upon him. 10 That is when I observed that lawless people were given burial, whereas others who had acted justly would come to the sanctuary and go away only to be soon forgotten in the city. That too is a breath. 11 For:

> Where no punishment is enacted,
> evil action is soon afoot,

For this reason, there arises in the human heart a desire to do evil. 12 For:

> A sinner can do evil a hundred times
> and afterward live long.

Of course I recall the saying:

> Those who fear God will prosper,
> because they fear before him;

29

13 The lawless will not prosper,
   and their life, like a shadow, does not last,
   because they do not fear before God.—

14 However, it has happened that things have been carried out upon
the earth that are a breath:
   there are law-abiding people
   to whom things happen
   as though their action were of a lawless person;
   and there are lawless people
   to whom things happen
   as though their action were of a law-abiding person.
From this I concluded that this too is a breath, 15 and I praised
joy: for there is no happiness for a person under the sun except to
eat and drink and be joyful, should this come to accompany a person in their labor during the days of life that God has given them
under the sun.

16 When I had set my mind to perceive what knowledge really is, and
to observe what business is really carried out on earth, 17 then I
observed, as to the whole of the action of God, that even if their
eyes never close in sleep, humans cannot find out what action is
being carried out under the sun. Thus humans really labor in
search of this but find nothing. Even if one who knows claims to
perceive it, he cannot find it. 9:1 For I have thought about all this
and examined it, and concluded: those who are law-abiding and
knowing, their actions are nevertheless in the hands of God. Such
a person never perceives whether he is loved or scorned; both
possibilities are standing before him. 2 Both—for everybody. The
same fate awaits the law-abiding and the lawless, the good, the
pure and the impure, those who offer sacrifice and those who do
not. It comes to the good as to the sinner, to those who swear
oaths as to those who are cautious about oaths. 3 What is evil, in
all that has been carried out under the sun, is that one and the
same fate awaits all. Moreover, in humans the heart is full of evil,
and their spirit is seized by delusion during their lifetime—and
afterward, as they are about to join the dead, 4 which one would
be exempted? For all the living, there happens to remain trust.
For:
   A living dog is better than a dead lion.

5 And: The living perceive that they will die; but the dead perceive
nothing at all. Moreover, they receive no further reward, because
their memory has been forgotten. 6 Love, hate, and envy toward
them have already disappeared. In all eternity they will never again
own a portion of anything that is carried out under the sun.

7 Go ahead, eat your bread with joy, and drink your wine with a
happy heart, for God long ago determined your activity as he
desired. 8 Always wear clean clothes, and care for your head with
hair creams. 9 Experience life with a woman you love, all the days
of your life of breath that he has given you under the sun, all your
days of breath. For that is your portion of life, and of the possessions for which you labor under the sun. 10 Everything that your
hand finds worth doing, do it, as long as you have the strength!
For there is neither action, nor accounting, nor perception, nor
knowledge in the netherworld to which you are going.

11 Again, I further observed under the sun that:
> The race does not go to the swift,
> victory in battle does not go to the powerful,
> nor does bread go to the knowledgeable,
> nor wealth to the clever,
> nor applause to the perceptive,
> since time and chance await each one.

12 Moreover, humans cannot perceive their appointed time.
> Like fish who are caught in an evil net,
> or birds caught in a snare,
> so every person is trapped in an evil time
> when suddenly it falls upon them.

13 And this too I observed under the sun: an example of knowledge
that I considered great: 14 There was a little city. It had few inhabitants. A great king marched against it. He surrounded it and built
great siege towers against it. 15 In the city there was found to be
a poor man who had knowledge. He saved the city through his
knowledge. Afterward, however, no one remembered this poor
man. 16 So I said:
> Knowledge is better than power;
> however, the knowledge of a poor man is discounted,
> and his words are not listened to.
>> 17 The cautious words of those who know are more acceptable
>> than the shouting of a boss among fools,
>> 18 and knowledge is better than weapons—
>> but a deviant individual can subvert much happiness.
>> 10:1 Dying flies—then stench and bubbles rise
>> in the creams of the perfumer;
>> a small stupidity proves more potent
>> than knowledge, than honor.
>> 2 The mind of one who knows takes to the right;
>> the mind of the fool takes the left;
>> 3 but the ignorant person—whichever way he walks,

31

the mind is not there,
though he has said of everyone else: he is ignorant.
4 If the boss is up in the air against you,
don't withdraw from your position;
for calmness cautions against
seriously deviant actions.
5 There happens an evil that I have observed under the sun—the
kind of oversight that tends to occur at the hands of an official:
6 Stupidity was placed on benches raised on high;
and wealthy people had to sit beneath them.
7 I observed slaves on horseback,
and princes walking on the earth like slaves.
8 One who digs a pit can fall into it;
the one who breaks through a wall, a snake might bite;
9 one who breaks stones can be wounded by them;
one who splits wood is endangered by that.
10 If the axe has become dull,
and its user has not sharpened it ahead of time,
then more muscle power is required—
he would have drawn profit from knowledge:
by having prepared his tool in advance.
11 If the snake bites
before he has charmed it,
the snake charmer
has no profit.
12 Words from the mouth of one who knows are applauded;
the lips of a fool bring him confusion.
13 The onset of words from his mouth is foolishness,
the consequence of his mouth is evil delusion.
14 And the ignorant person talks on and on. But humans do not perceive what is about to occur. And what will happen even after
that—who can tell? 15 The labor of the foolish will exhaust them,
since they do not perceive how to make their way in the city.
16 Woe to you, O land whose king is a slave,
and whose princes feast in the morning
17 Blessed are you, O land whose king is from noble stock
and whose princes schedule their eating
for self-control rather than carousing.
18 If one is slack, the framework sags,
if one drops one's hands, the house leaks.
19 One feasts in order to laugh,
and wine gives joy to the living,
and money is involved in both.

20 Even in your thoughts, don't badmouth a king;
   even in your bedroom, don't ridicule a wealthy person;
   for a bird of the heavens can project your voice,
   the winged one can broadcast the words.
11:1 Set your bread afloat upon the water,
   for after many days you will find it again.
2 Divide your capital seven or even eight ways,
   because you do not perceive what evil will occur in the land.
3 If the clouds swell with rain,
   they will pour it out on the land;
   if a tree falls toward the south, or toward the north,
   wherever the tree falls, that is where it will be.
4 One who gapes at the blowing air will not sow;
   one who stands observing the clouds will not reap.
5 Just as you cannot perceive the blowing air any more than the development of a child in a pregnant womb, so can you not perceive the action of God, who enacts everything. 6 In the morning begin to plant, and also toward evening do not let your hand rest, since you cannot perceive which will succeed, the one or the other. Or maybe both together will have a happy outcome.
7 Then will the light be sweet,
   and happy for the eyes to see the sun.
8 Because, even when a human being has many years of life,
   one should be joyful in each of them;
   and one should remember the days of darkness:
   they will be many.
   Everything that comes (into the world) is a breath.
9 Be joyful my boy, in your early days;
   have a happy heart during your boyhood.
   Get along on the paths where your heart leads you,
   toward the visions your eyes put before you.
[But perceive that God will bring you to judgment for all of that.]
10 Keep your mind free of vexation,
   and protect your body from evil,
   for youth and dark hair are a breath.
12:1 Remember your Creator in your early days,
   prior to when the days of evil come,
   and those years overtake you
   of which you will say: I have no interest in them;
2 prior to when the sun and the light and the moon and the
      stars go dark
   and the clouds return, even after the rainfall:
3 the day when the guards of the house tremble,

33

and the strong men are bent,
and the grinders give up, because they are too few,
and the women peering through the windows darken,

4 and the doors on the street are shut;
when the rumble of the mill is muted
the birdsong soars—
all the singers are bowed low;

5 also they fear the exalted one
because terrors lurk on the road;
the almond tree blossoms,
the locust plods along,
the caper berry bursts,
but a human being goes to his eternal home,
and the mourners circle through the streets.

6 Yes, prior to when the silver cord is loosed,
the golden bowl is shattered,
the jar on the well is smashed,
the broken wheel falls into the crater,

7 the dust returns to the earth as it was,
and the air returns to God who gave it.

8 "A breath, a puff of breath," this man named Qoheleth used
to say, "all are a breath."

9 Qoheleth was a man of knowledge. But even more he taught the
people the art of perception. He listened, and tested, and he
straightened out many a proverb. 10 Qoheleth sought to find interesting sayings, and these true sayings are here painstakingly
recorded.

11 The sayings of those who know are like goads,
like driven pegs are the words of writers of collections—
both are wielded by one and the same shepherd.

12 From more collecting, my son, be warned. Even if there is never
an end to the activity of making book after book, and much study
ruins one's health, 13 after all has been heard, the final word
would only be:
Fear God and keep his commandments!
For that is everything for humankind. 14 For God brings every
activity to judgment, every hidden thing, whether good or evil.

Title and Prologue

Title of the Book 1:1

1:1 The words of Qoheleth, the son of David, who was king in Jerusalem.

1:12; Prov 1:1; 1 Kgs 8:1

[1:1] This title must have been added to the book later. Its purpose is to associate the author, known in the book as "Qoheleth," with the prototype of all the wise men of Israel, namely Solomon, if not to intimate gingerly Qoheleth's identity with him. The material connection is built upon the royal tale in 1:12ff. The information in 1:12 is completed with the phrase "son of David" taken from Prov 1:1; and the name *Qoheleth* may possibly evoke in the minds of readers of the Hebrew Bible the fact that, according to 1 Kgs 8:1, Solomon assembled (*yaqhēl*) in Jerusalem all the ancients of Israel, and all the heads of the tribes. The purpose in making this connection was also achieved: the book joined the ranks of the official books of the Jewish religious community. For conjectures about how this may have come about in detail, see the Introduction, pp. 11–13.

Prologue 1:2-3

2 "A breath, a puff of breath . . . a breath, a puff of breath," Qoheleth used to say, "they all are a breath." 3 What profit does one draw from all the possessions for which one labors under the sun?

|| 12:8; Job 7:16; Ps 39:6; 62:10 ↗ Rom 8:20 *to 1:3:* 2:11, 18-22; 3:9; 5:15, 17; 8:9; 9:9

Overview of 1:2—2:2

Like a formal dinner, which offers a tasty series of various courses prior to the main course, or like a classical sonata, which rapidly runs through its major themes before presenting the first movement, so the book begins with a lengthy approach through the first, and into the second, section, before getting to a broad and continuous development. In terms of literary form, there comes first a formally presented saying of Qoheleth in 1:2, then a (rhetorical?) question in 1:3 (does Qoheleth himself speak here?), then an expanded poem objectively describing the world in 1:4-11, and finally, in 1:12—2:2, a subjectively stylized first-person narrative (now clearly he himself is speaking) concerning experiences and the thoughts derived from them, which, however, merely outlines in three brief glimpses what is yet to come. The real presentation begins only in 2:3. The nonlinear character of this writing, forever beginning anew, is mirrored by its content: important motifs of the book such as "breath," "profit," "possessions," and "under the sun," are briefly heard here to be later taken up once again. The literary technique of beginning with a slogan or summary (see Amos 1:2; Prov 1:2-6, 7; Isa 1:2-31; Ps 1) is further developed here in the spirit of the Cynic-Stoic diatribe. It is not interested in the objective and logical development of a thought, but rather about using all means to bring something home to the reader. Shock therapy, along with attention-getting suggestions, are employed to induce the appropriate expectations.

Notes on 1:2-3

[1:2] After 1:1 we would expect Qoheleth to be the speaker. But an unidentified authorial person speaks, and he cites Qoheleth. Without 1:1 we would have to say: "he is citing a leader of the assembly." It is as though we had turned on the radio in the middle of a program—the quoted text puts the reader in the middle of a speech, or even at the last sentence. One does not know to what the "all" refers. In terms of form, 1:2 is an ancient, festive, three-step parallelism (see Ps 93:3), which first emphasizes the word "breath," and then, by inversion, emphasizes "all." And the meaning of "breath" is not univocal. In the lament psalms, "breath" is an image of the ephemeral character of human life, its brevity, the fruitlessness of its striving (like shadows or wilting flowers). A similar meaning is found in the wisdom literature, both in Israel and in surrounding cultures.[1] Moreover, in the Deuteronomistic writings, "breath" had become a designation for false gods, idols. What does it mean here? On the tongue of which leader of the assembly? An expression of what? Verse 2 throws readers into a world whose conceptual system invites them, and yet remains cloaked in darkness.

---

[1] Among the Greeks, *typhos* corresponds to "wind," "smoke," "vapor." The Cynic philosopher Monimus is cited as saying that *typhon einei pan*, "everything is smoke." Reported in Diogenes Laertius, *Lives of Eminent Philosophers* 6.83; see R. D. Hicks, trans., LCL (Cambridge: Harvard Univ. Press, 1950). But in the popular philosophy it had been given an anthropological twist: "dimness, blindness."

[1:3] Verse 3 is connected by a linkword, which helps clarify a first question: "all—all the possessions." But whose words now appear, those of the author or those of the assembly leader, whom he cites—that remains unclear. The language is suddenly banal, with expressions from the marketplace, or from the merchant's stall ("profit," "possession"). The sentence mutters along in prosaic form. When everything seems to have been said, still it goes on (where do we live and work, if not "under the sun?"). The style probably breaks a taboo, in that street language and, possibly, intellectual jargon in a Greek mode are here juxtaposed to the most elevated style. Behind "profit" one can discern *ophelos*, a Greek word often used by authors who were read in the schools; with "under the sun" we hear the *hyph' hēliō* of school writers (in normal Hebrew, they wrote "under the heavens")—it is like the German written by journalists and intellectuals today, in which English idioms can be detected.

The "possessions" for which it "labors" is an etymological figure of speech (*ʿămālo šeyyaʿămōl*) that may perhaps mirror the phrase used by Euripedes and others, *mochthon mochthein*, "to take painful pains."[2] Unfortunately, the English translation cannot do justice to this figure here and anywhere else it occurs. The root word in Hebrew denotes both our laborious work and its result, the possessions. In our translation the two aspects are divided between the main clause and the subordinate clause. Where the original text has only the noun, the translation will be "labor" (4:4, 6; 6:7; 8:15; 10:15). The opening question, 1:3, although it is clearly a question from the perspective of ruling classes who own and multiply possessions, refers explicitly to humankind. Thus it turns to the human race in general, and it simply presupposes that humans are essentially laborious beings, intent upon possessions: *homo faber*. The formulation is so open that it does not permit being limited to individuals: technical humanness, which modifies and thus takes possession of the whole earth, is included within the category. It asks (at this point we are not sure whether the question is real or rhetorical) what "advantage" or "profit" results from such a way of being human. If work brings possession, what then does possession bring? Indeed, "all" possession: all possible success in human mastering of the world taken together. "Under the sun" makes the question still more basic: no reachable space in the cosmos is excluded, the cosmos being taken in terms of the image that ancient cultures had of it. The question's horizon is the world as such. This is a reality filled with light ("sun"), and yet within it there remains, for humans,

---

[2] See, e.g., Euripides, *Andromache* §134, and *Helen* §1446 (see Arthur S. Way, trans., LCL [reprint Cambridge: Harvard Univ. Press, 1959).

the question of meaning. Was a preemptive answer given already in 1:2? Will it now be answered immediately? The word "profit" does not occur again until 2:11, where the question of 1:2 is answered in the negative. But this is still only a first indication. An answer appears in argumentative context first in 2:22 (without the word "profit") and again in 3:9, and in both cases once again in the form of a question.

Cosmology

Change, Permanence, and Forgetting 1:4-11

4 A generation passes, another comes,
   the earth stays in eternity.

1:4-11: 3:11-15;
↗ Sir 14:18

5 The sun, which rose and then set,
   breathless it races back to the place where it rises again.

6 Southward blowing, and turning to the north,
   turning, turning, blows the air,
   and because it turns, the air returns.

7 All the streams flow to the sea;
   the sea does not fill—
   to the place whence the streams flow
   there they return to flow again.

8 All things are constantly restless,
   more than humans can express:
   the eye is not sated by observing;
   the ear is not filled by hearing.

4:8; 5:9; 8:17;
Prov 27:20

9 Whatever has occurred, that will occur again.
   What has been carried out, that will be carried out again.
   There is nothing new under the sun.

3:15; 6:10; 4:13-16

10 At times something happens about which they say:
    "Observe that—that is new"—
    but it has already occurred in the eternities
    that have gone before us.

11 There is no memory of the former ones;
    and of the future ones, still to come,
    there will also be no memory of them
    among those who will come after them.

2:16; 9:5; Isa 41:4

1:8 Another possible translation: "Human words are overstrained; no one can express it all."
1:10 Another possible translation: "But for ages there had already existed what has happened before our eyes."

Overview of 1:4-11

The poem that now suddenly begins is a cosmology, placed within the context of the question opened in 1:3: "humans in the cosmos." As a coherent structure of language expressing an affirmation, it clearly sets itself off from the question in 1:3. It begins by gathering observable realities, calmly described, that associate step by step the four elements of ancient cosmology and then come to humankind. At that point is presented the unifying thesis in 1:9 (here the linkphrase "under the sun" reappears), which is then developed through a concluding discussion in the form of an objection and its answer. The dynamic in the form of the poem consists in the constant reoccurrence, in ever lengthier units, of the opposition "change—identity remaining in spite of the change" (v. 4 = 2 lines; v. 5 = 2 lines; v. 6 = 3 lines; v. 7 = 4 lines; vv. 8-11 = 15 lines). This dynamic, which of itself tends to unlimited extension, is caught and tied down by a fixed strophic form that also comes into play: after two 2-line units there follows a sequence of one 3-line and two 4-line units. This sequence is then repeated in vv. 9-11, so that with v. 11 (within the unified expression of vv. 9-11 that exceeds the strophic measures) there is a possibility of an ending. This announces itself positively in that the content of v.11 links back to v. 4, and in this way forms a frame. Apart from this very subtle formal structuring of the poem, there are other levels of association, onomatopoeia, repetition, and play upon imagery, which the English translation has not always carried over. The greatest difficulty for modern readers of this poem is that our spontaneous reaction, in the face of its continuous assertion of the eternal return of the same, is to judge that this is a negative and depressing message. If we cannot break free of this prejudice, then we simply miss the entry into the poem. The poem praises the cosmos as glorious and eternal in this image of cyclic return. According to Greek sensibility, a reader would consider whether pantheism was implied. Humans, not as persons but in their activities, share in it also, because their activities always recur. Moreover, humans may speak about the cosmos. Humans do not perdure as subjects, however, and so we cannot unify in our experience and in our memory the extensions in space and time of being. As in all cyclic theory, from ancient myth through the Stoics to Nietzsche, what is at stake here is an analysis of the being in time of humans, an analysis that refuses to define this being as simply falling into nothingness.

Notes on 1:4-11

[1:4] Through the abstract concept "generation" a striking image is made possible for the fact that continuously humans die and others are born. The ancients imagined the world as a fixed disk upon which there existed a space that "one generation" left and another entered. The point being made is the "eternity" of the cosmos ("eternity" is also a liturgical formula).

[1:5] The sun, which sets, appears to be transient like humans, but it is not. It rises unchanged in its cycle—in the ancient imagination this is expressed as a speedy return during the night. Thus it too is "forever."

[1:7] This sentence also looks to the notion of cycle. Some speech elements in 1:5 and 1:6 also signal this: they are found again at the end of 1:7.

[1:8] The first line here evokes the first line of 1:7. For this reason, *děbārîm* (which can denote both "thing" and "word") must be understood as an encompassing signifier of everything in the cosmos. See Menander: "For all things exert themselves within their duration."[1]

In line 2 "express" (*lĕdabbēr*) picks up the root word, but now in an anthropological sense. Humankind links up with the four elements (earth, fire, air, water), in that it unites "what is" to itself through language. As language is ordered to meaning, and meaning is far from being adequate to the fullness of cosmic events, humans never come to the end of their task in speaking.

[1:9] The first line summarizes the teaching of eternal return for the cosmos. As the relation of humans to the cosmos is fixed in v. 8, here line 2 draws the conclusion (poetically: through parallelism) that eternal return also includes identical forms of human activity. (3:2-8 can provide some examples of this.) Line 3, as negatively formulated, gives a final, triumphal, universality. "New" is here a negative word. In a world of unending duration and return, what is "new" could only be worse—but then there is no such thing.

[1:10] For the first time in the book there appears an opposed view. This will often happen again. Here it is almost too clearly introduced. That

---

[1] See *Flor.* 29.19 in J. Stobaeus, *Anthologium*, ed. Curtius Wachsmuth and Otto Hense (Berlin: Weidman, 1884–1912). In the case of Menander, it is not always possible to refer to available English publications since editions and fragment numbers of this author are currently in flux.

will frequently not be the case later. The opposed view: in fact, experience always presents something "new." In vv. 10b-11 the opposed view is answered in its own terms. If it is true that in v. 9 "new" connotes "worse," however, then it could be that we are hearing now, for the first time, the voices of some of Qoheleth's interlocutors; see later, especially 7:10. They have a pessimistic philosophy of history, perhaps representing the beginnings of apocalyptic. According to them, the world just gets worse and worse.

[1:11] How the opposed view of 1:10 could arise must be explained. As only human activities return, while those who carry them out do not remain identically the same, therefore no abiding or growing common human awareness can take form: memory is constantly breaking down.[2]

---

[2] Simonides, the lyric songwriter, already expressed this observation in the time of the Persian wars. See *Greek Lyric* §§581 and 594, ed. and trans. David A. Campbell, LCL (Cambridge: Harvard Univ. Press, 1991) 3:464–65, 472–73.

Anthropology

Three Previews 1:12—2:2

12 I am Qoheleth. I was king over Israel in Jerusalem. 13 I had made up my mind to examine and to explore, with the help of knowledge, whether all that is carried out under the heavens is really a bad business in which humankind is forced to be involved, at a god's command. 14 I observed all the actions that are carried out under the sun. The conclusion: all are a breath, an inspiration of air.

> 15 What is bent cannot be straightened;
> what is not there cannot be counted.

16 I thought to myself as follows. Look: I have increased and expanded my knowledge, so that now I have surpassed everyone who has ruled over Jerusalem before me. I have often been able to observe knowledge and perception. 17 So I took upon myself to perceive what knowledge really is, and to perceive what delusion and ignorance really are. I perceived that this also is a spirit of air. 18 For

> Much knowledge—much vexation;
> deeper perception—deeper pain.

2:1 I said to myself, Go ahead, try being joyful, taste happiness. The conclusion: that too is a breath.

> 2 About laughter I said: What nonsense!
> About joy: What good is it?

Marginal references:

1:1
3:1, 10; 8:9, 16f; 5:13

2:11; 4:4

1:8; 3:14; 7:13; Prov 27:22

2:7, 9; 1Kgs 5:9f; 10:7, 23

2:12; 7:25; 8:16f

2:18; +2:23; 5:16
Prov 2:15

2:3, +10, 24; 3:12;
↗ Wis 2:6
10:19; Prov 14:13;
20:1; 23:29-35

Overview of 1:12—3:15

Wide-ranging prose dominates this segment of the text. It was already heard in 1:3. Now it is interrupted sometimes with proverbs, with an argumentative insertion (2:14), or with conclusions to an argument (1:15, 18; 2:2; perhaps 3:15). Sometimes it builds enumerations into half-poetic passages (2:4-8; 3:2-8; perhaps 2:23). Its subject matter is a question about humanity that leads to a question about God. It is the most basic, and most coherent, development of the book. It does not by any means present itself as an objective and cool statement and analysis of facts, but rather as one person's account of his career, his success, his reflections on it, and his conclusions. This narrative form leaves the reader free to compare his/her own life with its experiences, and to accept its logic only after critical examination.

A subtle playing with the identity of the narrator further extends the free space for the reader. Whereas between 1:3 and 1:11 it remained unclear just whose words were heard, whether it was the authorial figure of 1:2 or a "leader of the assembly" quoted by the author, so now in 1:12 the author is free to identify himself as this "leader of the assembly." He had not dared, until now, to take it upon himself outright—but now he does. At the same moment, however, he veils himself once again by the literary technique of a royal make-believe, a masquerade in which he assumes the image of a philosopher king of Jerusalem, the famous Solomon (see especially the references to 1 Kgs 1:4-8); and yet he is not Solomon (see Qoh 1:6; 2:7, 9: in Israel's historical memory Solomon had only one single predecessor in Jerusalem—his father, David—not many). The royal robe then sinks imperceptibly to the floor; its last appearance is in 2:25. Still, Solomon's project in 1:3 begins to be answered only in 3:10, and so the royal masquerade may be thought truly to end only in 3:15.

Through use of this masquerade in which a person is presented in a higher social level, it is possible, without forfeiting the advantages of narrative presentation, to base an anthropology not on the experiences of people who fail to grow or to achieve anything in life, but rather on the experiences of the highest human possibility, in the most fortunate world situations, joyfully lived. This makes only more devastating what then appears: the inevitable approach of death, the uncontrollable freedom of others regarding that world reality which I have shaped, and the uncontrollability of joy even for those who have brought about all its conditions for themselves.

This leads humankind to the basic option of despair—although humans must hold on to the truth that everything that happens in this human world, though we cannot see it, is made perfect and eternal from God. Here a circle is completed back to 1:4-11, with the difference that while the perspective came from the cosmos alone there, here a theological dimension is added. This dialectic between anthropology and theology distinguishes Qoheleth from most of the modern existential philosophers, although in other respects their analyses come astonishingly close to his.

To understand the apparently very loose prose of Qoheleth, it is important to realize that it is also very tightly held together and united through the use of linkwords, advance announcements, resumptions, associations and linking through opposites (all of which only in exceptional cases can be pointed out in what follows). Much can be understood only when the reader also recalls things said earlier, and when the interpretation remains open to still later resumption of the topic.

At first the narrative is still summarized and abrupt: three notices about an undertaking that was begun, but each time an immediate reference to its result and a conclusion in the form of a saying. Subsequently the reader perceives that Solomon/Qoheleth was giving only previews here of what he will then narrate fully and coherently in 2:3—3:15.

The relationship between the previews and the full narratives is marked on two levels: first, more superficially, by the recurrence of a specific sequence of words from 1:12—2:2 in 2:3-26; and then once again, shortened, in 3:1-15. The linkword sequence is *twr,* "explore" (1:13; 2:3) —*baḥokmâ,* "with the help of/the knowledge" (1:13; 2:3) —*ʿśh,* "is carried out," "bring about," "take action" (1:13; 2:3; 3:9)—*taḥat haššāmayim,* "under the heavens" (1:13; 2:3; 3:1)—*libnê hāʾādām,* "humankind," "humans" (1:13; 2:3; 3:10)—*ḥokmâ,* "knowledge" (1:17; 2:12)—*hôlēlôt,* "delusion" (1:17; 2:12)—*wěsiklût,* "and ignorance" (1:17; 2:12)—*śimḥâ,* "joy" (2:1, 26; 3:12)—*rʾh,* "taste," "observe" (2:1, 24; 3:13)—*ṭôb,* "happy," "happiness," "blessed" (2:1, 24-26; 3:12-13). This recurring sequence shows at least that this should be a coherent text. It will further become clear that something new begins in some way with 3:1. Not by linkword sequence but rather by content, 2:3-26 can be divided into two smaller sections: 2:2-10 and 2:11-26.

However, the relationship between the contents of the three previews and the three full narratives has a chiastic form. 1:13-15 first announces the closing "theological" section of the narrative (3:1-15); then 1:16-18 announces the middle section, which contains the anthropological development properly so called (2:11-26); finally 1:1-2 announces the foundational section that follows immediately, in which Solomon/Qoheleth proves, through a report on his own experience, that it is possible for humans to shape the world through their knowledge and so come to good fortune.

The chiastic relationship of the contents of the three previews can be clearly seen in their formulations—almost to the correspondence of whole sentences. See especially 2:3, 10 (for at least 2:3-10) with 2:1-2 ("joy," "happiness"); 2:12 (for at least 2:12-17) with 1:17; and 3:1, 9-10, prepared in 2:26, (for 3:1-15) with 1:13-14. The repetition of linkwords from 1:18 in 2:22 expands the field of reference of 1:16-18 to 2:12-23. For further details see the verse-by-verse commentary.

Later passages in the book, of course, also link back to formulations from 1:12—2:2. The closing sayings in 1:15, 18; 2:2 were perhaps already familiar to the readers, but this cannot be documented. Most probably 2:2b has been reformulated.

When the readers are carried into the first-person narrative through 1:12—2:3 they probably should arrive deeply impressed by the word "breath." Even the preview announcement (1:13-15) of the theological developments, in which after 2:26 the word "breath" does not occur, is shaped in such a way as to climax (1:14) in the "breath" formula. So at this point, despite the preview, the reader does not suspect that a very positive theology will seize upon so negative an anthropology.

Notes on 1:12—2:2

[1:12] The text in this verse corresponds to the style of royal documents, which begin with a self-presentation and then they start the narrative. The original readers may have had this sense of the sentence. Thus the royal narrative mode is expressed at the level of form as well.

[1:13] In the word "explore" (Hebrew *tûr;* see Greek *tērein,* which was an important word for the post-Socratic empirical schools, and which also sounds similar for Semitic ears keyed to the consonants) the influence of Greek language is felt; and the language of commerce in the phrase "bad business" (see 5:13). There is a play on words between "bad business" (ʿinyan rāʿ) and "forced to be involved" (ʿny). "Knowledge," and not the usual "wisdom," is the more exact translation in Qoheleth for the Hebrew *ḥokmâ.* Sometimes "education" or "culture" is appropriate. This is true for the whole book. The opposed concepts are stupidity, ignorance, knowing nothing, but not madness. It deals with that knowledge and skill which can be converted into technique and mastery, and that education which leads to social standing. See 2:3-10; 2:13-17; etc. Hellenism had imposed itself because it possessed new and more intelligent military strategies, more sophisticated methods in commercial bookkeeping and governmental administration, and more advanced methods in farming and in the production of handcrafts. All that is "knowledge" and "skill" in the thought of Qoheleth. Of course the word *ḥokmâ* means for him sometimes ultimate knowledge, questioning of deepest realities, "philosophy." So too here in v. 13. Qoheleth had a thesis in mind with which he disputes. For the second time, after 1:10, others are cited—this time not in direct, but in indirect, discourse. It may be the same group as in v. 10. Their thesis may originate in Greek culture (see the formulation "a god") or else from early apocalyptic circles in Israel itself. In any case they found only evil in everything under the heavens.

Just as in 1:3, the question is about the meaning of the whole of what happens through humankind in the world. What is new is that here, in this sketch of a possible thesis, the sphere of "god" (*ʾĕlōhîm*) is introduced. That happens here for the first time in the book, and not yet as a formulation of Qoheleth himself. Because of the passive formulation "all that is carried out under the heavens," the original readers could come to the question whether human enterprise, which was clearly meant, was not to be understood at the same time as something with which God too was involved. It may not be by accident that Qoheleth does not say "under the sun" here, but rather "under the heavens." He is already drawing the reader here toward God, about whom the text will immediately speak. See 5:1: "God is in heaven, you are on the earth." The same is true of the passive formulations in the whole book. To this degree Qoheleth himself approaches the discourse about God, and the possibility of a pantheistic interpretation of 1:4-11 is put aside.

If Qoheleth throughout the book speaks only of "God," without ever using the ancient name "Yahweh" for God, this is easily understood hundreds of years after the establishing of monotheistic thinking in Israel, and in a context in which, on the one hand, there is a rising wariness about using the name Yahweh, and, on the other hand, this name is more and more abused in popular magic. We must also take into account a certain formulaic pressure from the language of Greek philosophers who made fun of polytheism. It is completely inappropriate, however frequently it is done, to conclude from the absence of God's name in the text to any cooling or depersonalizing of Qoheleth's relation to God. In any case, what is special about 1:13 is that "a god" is very vaguely spoken of—this is not Qoheleth's idea, however, but rather an idea that he wanted to examine. See the text that begins in 3:1, especially after 3:10. Here he carries out his examination.

[1:14] The expression translated "an inspiration of air," used in tandem with or in place of "breath," is hard to translate. Drawing on Hos 12:1

(MT 12:2) many translate it "herding of wind" or else "snatching at wind." But in Qoheleth's Hebrew, *rĕʿût rûaḥ* and *raʿyôn rûaḥ* are interchangeable (1:17; 4:16). The second word occurs also in 2:22 in the expression *raʿyôn lēb,* where it can mean only "the thinking, striving, stretching out of the mind." Thus *rĕʿût rûaḥ* could mean "windy, airy thinking; ineffectual longing." We are dealing with a loanword from Aramaic, which makes sense in Middle Hebrew. This was always taken to be the case by Jewish exegetes in the medieval period and by Christians on into the nineteenth century.

[1:15] Line 1 suggests the bent back of an old man—the subtext is an early reference to death. Line 2 is taken once again from the merchant's table, recalling the "bad business" of 1:13, and its thought will be taken up again in 3:14. Line 2 can just as well be applied to farmers who, because of a meager harvest in the autumn, cannot manage to deliver their dues to their lords and to the government. Both sayings touch on the theme of what lies beyond our control, which theme will become dominant in the theological section from 3:1 on. In 7:13 line 1 will be cited, but God will be the subject of the verb.

[1:16-18] Qoheleth's reflections in v. 16 continue into v. 17a. Verses 16-18 are clearly a streamlined preview of 2:12-26. First the results of the foregoing pericope, 2:3-10, are indicated with formulations from 2:9 (1:16). Then the question that arises from this result is formulated using phrases from 2:12 (1:17a). The argumentation that follows 2:12 is represented only by the "inspiration of air" conclusion (1:17b: see 2:15, 17, 19, 21, 23, and especially 2:22). Finally 1:18 rehearses linkwords from 2:23. From this concentrated referring of 1:16-18 to 2:12-26 the analogy can be made to 1:13-15 and 1:12, where the preview character is less marked but is similarly indicated by linkwords. It is from this that the reader can see the chiastic structure mentioned above.

[1:18] The saying, probably already familiar, deals with a theme of ancient school masters: they would make clear to their students that without effort, pain (including punishment), worry, and vexation, they would never achieve knowledge and a penetrating intelligence. See our saying, "No pain, no gain." The motifs of "pains" and "care" will be taken up again in a very different manner (2:23; 5:16), and at that point this saying will be heard again in a different light.

[2:1-2] After the structure has been put in place, the third preview can be very brief, and basically introduce the theme of the first full development, which follows immediately. Moreover, the author can change the form slightly. Instead of simply adding a full-blown saying (1:15), or introducing it with "For," here he provides full introductory phrases and suggests the sayings in shortened form. Loud laughter is not appropriate in a cultured person (see 7:6). Then as a parallel is a skeptical saying about joy (also with a merchant's dismissive tone). In this way joy is compared to laughing and thus discounted. At the same time the question about the "profit of profits" is recalled, which was heard in 1:3 and will be addressed at the beginning of a new unit in 2:11, though the word "profit" of 1:3 and 2:11 is not used here.

Human Happiness through Shaping a New World 2:3-10

3 I drove myself to exploration in order to bathe my body in wine. And my mind kept leading my knowledge to pasture in order to imprison ignorance until I might observe what kind of happiness   +2:1
humans can bring about under the heavens during the few days of their lives. 4 I expanded my action:

> I built houses for myself;   1 Kgs 7
> I planted vineyards for myself.   Song 8:11

5 I set out gardens and parks for myself;   Song 4:13
> in them I planted all sorts of trees.   Gen 2:5

6 I arranged overflowing ponds,   Neh 2:14
> so as to water the stands of sprouting trees.

7 I bought male and female slaves,   1 Kgs 10:5
> although I already owned house slaves.
> I owned also a large number of animals, cattle, sheep, and   1 Kgs 5:3; 8:63
> > goats,
> more than all those who preceded me in Jerusalem.   1:16; 2:9; 1 Kgs 10:23

8 I collected silver and gold for myself as well   1 Kgs 10:21
> and, as my personal possession, kings and provinces.   1 Kgs 5:1-8
> I procured singers, male and female, trained for me,   2 Sam 19:36
> and what a man desires: a large harem.   1 Kgs 11:3

9 I was already great, and I increased even more, so that I sur-   1:16; 2:7; 1 Kgs 10:23
passed all those who preceded me in Jerusalem. Moreover, my   1 Kgs 5:9-14
knowledge remained with me, 10 and whatever my eyes desired I   2:1, 10, 24; 3:12, 22;
did not withhold from them. I did not have to deny my heart any   5:17f; 8:15; 9:6, 7-9;
joy. For my heart could draw joy from all my possessions. And that   11:7-10
was my portion out of all my possessions.

2:3 The construction and meaning of the MT is not easy to unravel.
2:8 Another possible translation: "and the personal tributes from kings and governors."—"A large harem": literally "a beloved, many beloveds." Meaning uncertain.

Overview of 2:3-10

With this unit there begins the ongoing narrative of Qoheleth/Solomon. He tells how he formed his royal life and world, through the application of his knowledge (outer frame motif in 2:3bα and 2:9b), and out of this "possession" as his "portion" he then had achieved that desired "joy" (2:10; see the motif of wine in 2:3 as a hint of banquet as the place of "joy"). That is the opening question in 2:3bβ: whether good fortune could be managed. The answer in 2:10 is a yes based on experience.

Verses 4-8 display almost poetically the world-conquering activity of the narrator. Framed by 2:4a and 9a (the inner frame formed of motifs of the "greatness" of the king), 5 + 5 finite verbs carry two series of affirmations: the king sets up his world (vv. 4b-6) and fills it with inhabitants and treasures (vv. 7-8). Undoubtedly the similar two-fold disposition (the world/its inhabitants) in the creation narrative in Genesis 1 stands in the background, as it does in Genesis 2. Genesis 2 is closer to the image of gardens and parks. Naturally Qoheleth also reaches back to 1 Kings 5–11 (Solomon!) and may well have made use also of traditional narrative lists in Greek literature.

Above all, however, he had concrete examples before his eyes. A distant model may have been the palace of the Lagids, and the surrounding area of parks, lakes, and public edifices in Alexandria. This covered a third of the territory of the city. Nearer at hand were the buildings and formal gardens of the Greek aristocracy upon properties either privately owned or held in fiefdom from the royal estate in Palestine, which the Jewish upper classes tried, in part successfully, to emulate. The high point would have been the Tobiad family, with their army and their mountain palace beyond the Jordan. The image sketched here is a literary attempt to express the passion of world conquest and world transformation that shook the Ptolemaic kingdom in the full flush of its founding years. If to us the picture seems bourgeois-private, we must note that the Ptolemaic notion of kingdom styled the state as a kind of immense private household. Thus it fully intends the public wealth, even though its prosperity is depicted only in the prosperity of the king. We are astonishingly close to the basic impetus of our own civilization: technical, world transforming, hungry for progress, especially the longing to maximize happiness. In Qoheleth, who otherwise writes as a cosmopolitan and allows very little to appear that is narrowly Israelite, it cannot be unintentional that the king who succeeds in transforming the world and maximizing happiness is specifically a king over Israel, in Jerusalem (1:12; 2:7, 9). Does he not express here the unquestioning conviction that good fortune can happen to the world only out of Jerusalem?

Notes on 2:3-10

[2:3] "in order to bathe my body with wine": exuberant description of the joys of a banquet. The supreme expression of human happiness is a banquet among friends, in which the flagon of wine is handed around—so it was in the ancient Orient and in the Hellenistic world. The two images "leading my knowledge to pasture" (for the use of Hebrew *b* with *nhg*, cf. Isa 11:6) and "imprison ignorance" are two sides of the same coin: to make full use of one's own knowledge and skill in order to construct a world in which happiness can be achieved. The usual interpretation (to give oneself over to foolishness, though moderated by wisdom) rests on inexact translation and does not fit either with the two pictures or with 2:9-10. What he really did follows in 2:4-8. The mention of "the few days" of human life gives the whole enterprise a somewhat pressured cast, but it also implicitly announces that all of this will prove to be "a breath."

[2:8] In documents from the second millennium B.C.E. vassal kings were already characterized as "personal possession" or as "privy purse" of the great king. Still the alternative translation, "personal tribute," although it is not so certain, may well be more fitting in the Hellenistic milieu. The whole kingdom was the *oikia* (household) of the king; everything that came to it was attributed personally to the king.

[2:10] "Portion" is in itself a concept from ancient Israelite real-estate law. In Qoheleth it has become a positive philosophical concept. But whether the "portion" that is possible for humans is also a "profit" remains a question. The very next sentence will strike a negative note, and the whole house of cards collapses.

Knowledge and Wealth as Fleeting 2:11-26

11 And I reflected on all the actions that my hands had carried out, and on the possessions that I had labored to possess. The conclusion: they are all a breath and an inspiration of air. There is no profit under the sun.   +1:3

12 I reflected, by observing what knowledge and what delusion and ignorance really are. Moreover, what kind of human will succeed the king whom they had earlier established? 13 I observed: yes, a profit comes from knowledge, and not from ignorance, just as there is a profit from light rather than from darkness: +1:17   6:8

14 One who knows has eyes in his head;
    a fool walks in darkness.

8:1; 10:2; Job 12:25
3:19; 9:2f; Job 9:22
7:16

But I perceived: Me too! For one and the same fate awaits each one. 15 So I thought to myself: the fate that awaits the fool also awaits me. Why then have I gathered knowledge beyond measure? And I said to myself that this too is a breath.

16 For there is no eternal memory of a person who knows, any more than of a fool, for in the days just ahead both will be forgotten.

+1:11; ⁄Wis 2:4
Ps 49:11

How can it be that the one who knows must die just like the fool? 17 And living became irksome to me, for the actions that are carried out under the sun weighed on me as an evil. Yes, all are a breath and an inspiration of air.

5:12, 15; 6:1f; 10:5

2:18f: 4:8
1 Kgs 12:1-17
to 2:18: 2:12, 21;
6:1-7; Ps 39:7

18 And also irksome to me were all my possessions for which I am laboring under the sun, and which I must leave behind for some human who will come after me. 19 Who perceives whether it will be one who knows or one who is ignorant? And yet someone will have power over all my possessions for which I have labored under the sun, and applied my knowledge. This too is a breath.

20 And then I turned to despair concerning all my possessions, for which I am laboring under the sun. 21 For it happens that the possessions which one person has accumulated through knowledge and perception and skill must be handed over as the portion of another person who has not labored for it. This too is a breath and a recurring evil.

6:2; ⁄ Sir 11:18f

6:1

+1:3

22 What then does a person get out of all one's possessions and by weaving plans in one's mind, in all one's labor under the sun?
    23 Day after day business consists only of pains and vexation;
        and even at night one's mind is not at rest.
    That too is a breath.

1:18; 5:16; 8:16f;
11:10; Job 7:1-4

+2:10

24 That happy disposition, whereby one can eat and drink and come to perceive happiness in one's possessions, is not a given in human nature. My observation has been rather that this comes from the hand of God. 25 For who, if not I, has something to eat, or is able to enjoy? 26 Now there are humans who are blessed in the eyes of God. They are the ones to whom he has given knowledge, and perception, and joy. And there are those whose life has failed. They are the ones whom he has commanded to be involved in the business of increasing and collecting, and then of giving it all to the one who is blessed in the eyes of God. That too is a breath and an inspiration of air.

7:26; Job 27:16f;
Prov 13:22; 28:8

Overview of 2:11-26

This unit, previewed in 1:16-18, is introduced by a kind of new preview in 2:11 that anticipates its disillusioning conclusion. "There is no profit" reaches all the way forward even into the theological section (3:9). 1:3 is answered here, but the answer is not yet based on an explanation. The whole section is constructed of a series of smaller units each ending in the "breath" expression. This expression was a structural signal as early as 1:13—2:2, though there it was always followed by a saying. Here the word "breath" in each case sums up the preceding intellectual activity. Thus 2:13—22 gives substance to the expression of 1:3. There are six units:

2:13-15	ending with "breath"
2:16-17	"breath" + "inspiration of air"
2:8-19	"breath"
2:20-21	"breath" + "evil"
2:22-23	"breath"
2:24-26	"breath" + "inspiration of air"

If one also takes into account the preview in 2:11 ("breath" + "inspiration of air"), there results in this important unit seven "breath" expressions, of which every other one is lengthened:

2:11	"breath" + "inspiration of air"
2:15	"breath"
2:17	"breath" + "inspiration of air"
2:19	"breath"
2:21	"breath" + "evil"
2:23	"breath"
2:26	"breath" + "inspiration of air"

This system of recurring endings distinguishes this unit from the theological unit, which follows and in which the "breath" expression does not occur at all (3:1-15). Even at this early point of the book, it is evident that what we read in the frame of the book about all being "breath" (1:2 and 12:8) is neither the whole, nor the most important part, of what the book has to say.

If in 2:21 the word "evil" replaces "inspiration of air," this has already been prepared in 2:17 ("weighed on me as an evil"). "Evil" in similar form will recur in 5:12-15; 6:1-2, where the case of 2:21 is further developed.

It is clear that the word "breath" serves here as a structural signal. These are very small structures. They are units that are intimately linked to one another. We therefore must not infer from this structure in this part of the book that "breath" necessarily functions as a structuring element in other parts of the book in the same way.

All the units separated by the "breath" formula discuss what, in the following notes, will be called "limit situations," using a term coined by the existentialist philosopher Karl Jaspers (*Grenzsituationen,* sometimes translated "boundary/borderline situations").

Notes on 2:11-26

[2:12] Anaphorically picking up on 2:11, this verse indicates the organization of the two segments that follow: 2:13-17 will put in question knowledge and culture, and from 2:18 the theme "successor" is taken up.

[2:13-17] If "knowledge" has at first been shown to be a condition for providing prosperity and happiness, this "profit" disappears in the sudden perspective of human limits, that is, certain death. Death is the first "limit situation" Qoheleth considers. One technique for repressing it is the consideration of fame, through which a person can live on after death. Recalling 1:11, 2:16 cuts off that technique. There arises the tone of a lament song: "How can it be?" Lament is a first yes, painful as it may be, to hard facts. It leads immediately to a new attitude. The Hebrew word (*śānē᾿tî*) includes everything that is opposed to love—from "hating" all the way down to something like "losing its appeal for me." On this scale our translation has chosen "be irksome," though it could be that nothing more was meant than that his previously habitual relationship with vigorous and involved living has been temporarily broken. Now living has become a burden. What once appeared to bring about good times (*ṭôb,* "happiness," "prosperity," 2:1, 3) now produces evil (*raʿ,* 2:17). Insofar as our happiness is mixed with unhappiness when we reflect on death, we humans transcend our fixation on success and pleasure.

[2:14-15] The words translated "fate" and "awaits" have the same root in Hebrew (*qrh*).[1]

---

[1] As a Greek example of this notion, very widespread in the ancient world, see Menander, §538: "These are the bones and unsubstantial dust of men who once were kings, of despots, of the wise, of men who plumed themselves on noble birth, on wealth, and on their fame and bodies beautiful. . . . Hades is the common lot of mortals all. Look thou on these and know thyself the man thou art" (*Menander: The Principal Fragments,* trans. F. G. Allison, LCL [New York: Putnam's Sons, 1930] 484–85).

[2:16] Until now death has been veiled, or spoken of in an abstract manner. Here, in the lament, the word "to die" is used for the first time.

[2:18-19] Through anaphora ("irksome to me"; see 2:17), the treatment of the theme "successor" (see 2:12) is made parallel to the foregoing text. The thought of death can similarly be repressed by consideration of one's work ("possessions") now as objective reality. Do the results of our working and of our creativity continue on, beyond an individual's lifetime? In our own day, whole nations are urged to ever greater sacrifice, so that coming generations might live in a better world. But the "limit situation" of "the other" removes this escape hatch. After my death the objective goods that I have put together are delivered to "others," whose capacities and even freedom escape any influence from me.

[2:20-23] The "limit situation" of "the other" regards not only what, after my death, will result from the world I made, but also possible events even before my death. It develops, then, into a further "limit situation" that Jaspers called "historicity." In his fictive autobiography, Qoheleth had supposed the best possible outcome, namely that happiness actually resulted for the one who had formed his/her world with knowledge and skill. But there is no necessary link from productive work to happiness. For this reason he now (2:21-23) introduces a common case, as a possibility that he had already been concerned with earlier in his imagined time of being king. It is the case where someone makes an effort, but the good resulting from this effort, even during one's lifetime, goes to another. Losing one's possessions during one's life time must be intended here, because the case of distributing possessions to heirs after one's death has already been dealt with, and 2:22-23 seem to consider a life continuing (unhappily now) while one's possessions have passed to another.

In this reflection the "king" here goes beyond his own experience, which he had first described in 2:3-10. Characteristic for that is the word yēš, "it happens," which in more than half of its occurrences brings the experience, first described here, again and again into ever new light (2:21; 5:12; 6:1; 7:15; 8:14; 10:5). What happens is described in the third person rather than in the first, for it is no longer Qoheleth's own experience.[2] Such things must have taken place in many upstanding third-

---

[2] For the experience itself, see Menander: "The one scrapes and saves honestly for himself; while the other, with malice, lays an ambush for the one who had long protected his possessions, and he triumphs" (*Die Komödien und Fragmente*, ed. G. Goldschmidt [Zurich: Artemis, 1949] §113).

century families in Judea, alienated as they were by foreign influence on all sides and threatened in their effort to climb commercial ladders. Such misfortunes led to debt slavery, as may be suggested in 2:23. Qoheleth will return to such experiences in later parts of the book (especially 5:12—6:10). Here he describes it briefly.

In 2:20, which parallels the introduction in 2:18, he introduces the unit by referring to a state of mind to which this process of thought has led him and which he, moreover, consciously assumes (2:20, "I turned to"). It is "despair" regarding all efforts and their results. Through it humans achieve a transcending distance from their own limited situation, even when the good times are there. Kierkegaard considered "despair" to be a "sickness unto death." Apparently here it is not depressing, but rather it opens one's eyes so that out of a discussion of "historicity" anthropology can become theology.

[2:24-26] The three "limit situations"—"inevitable death," "the others," "historicity"—profoundly modify the "happiness" that comes to the king/Qoheleth, as soon as they enter his mind. Just the same, "happiness" is not a given. He must return to the topic of "happiness." He must ask from whom and how it comes to him, insofar as it does come. That is where the transition to the theological section begins—still within the preceding section. This transition opens with a thesis.

The reflection has come to be so dominant in the meantime that it is now hard to say whether Qoheleth in v. 24a is recalling a thought that crossed his mind during his imagined royal period, or whether he is speaking out of his present narrative moment. However, the following sentences indicate that he is still reporting his earlier thought.

After the thesis and the introduction of the themes of happiness and of God, he goes back to his experience in 2:20-23, which he now reformulates in theological terms. It is important to note that Qoheleth does not in some way infer God from the "historicity" of humans, but rather he begins with God, whose presence he takes for granted as the real mover in all that happens, and treats "historicity" as coming from God.

In 2:25, the last grammatical trace of the royal fiction, the objectivity of the speaker is underlined: out of his own experience he might well not have had to state it so drastically, since he always experienced success and good fortune. But then, in 2:26, he writes the troubling sentence about God's rule over this world, outside all our moral expectations. There are *theophiloi*, "friends of God," as the Greeks expressed it at that time, and other men and women for whom the circumstances of their life do not come to a good end. God does not rule the world by cause and effect and moral principles, as humans would expect. Thus, even after the theological dimension has been opened, the repeated summary refrain holds true: even the distribution of good fortune and bad fortune is a breath.

In the meantime, the notion of "breath" has become clear to the reader. It looks to fleetingness, inevitable death, the uncertain linkage between effort and enjoyment of its fruits—in short, the amoral character of the world's unfolding. However, one could translate it as "meaninglessness" or "absurdity" only in a very preliminary sense, because Qoheleth poses the question of ultimate "meaning" only from 3:1 on, after God has been introduced into the picture. After 2:26 the "breath" formula completely disappears until the end of the theological section.

With the formulation of a "business" in which humans have "been involved" by God, Qoheleth is quoting the expression of other people whose opinion he, according to 1:13, intended to investigate. He begins this investigation right here. What he must establish, at least preliminarily, is a category division: the affirmation of 1:13 does not include all individual persons, but only a specific group, namely those "whose life has gone astray"; moroever, Qoheleth does not speak here of a "bad" business. He will return to the question in 3:10.

God's Action Inscrutable in Its Fullness 3:1-15

3:1 Everything has its hour. For every interest under the heavens there is an appointed time:

1:13; 3:17; 8:5f;
9:11f; 11:9; Ps 31:16

2 A time to give birth
and a time to die;
a time to plant,
and a time to harvest the plants;

7:17; Job 5:26
Isa 28:23-29

3 a time to kill
and a time to heal;
a time to tear down
and a time to build;

4 a time to cry
and a time to laugh;
a time of lament
and a time of dance;

5 a time to throw stones
and a time to gather stones;
a time to embrace
and a time to stay arm's length;

6   a time to search
    and a time to give up for lost;
    a time to keep
    and a time to throw away;
7   a time to tear
    and a time to sew;
    a time to be silent

Prov 15:23   and a time to speak;

9:1, 6   8   a time to love
                  and a time to hate;
                  a time of war
                  and a time of peace.

+1:3   9   When anyone takes action, what profit does he make from his
                 labor?

+1:13   10 I had now observed the business in which humans are forced to
11:5; 3:14f   be involved because of a god's command. 11 All that, he has
7:14, 23-29; 8:16f enacted perfectly in its time. Moreover he has put eternity in all of
Ps 139:13-18   it, but not in such a way that humans could find out the action
Sir 39:16   which God has carried out from its beginning to its end.

+2:10   12 I perceived that in all of it there is no happiness in activities,
                 except insofar as one can be joyful and in this way enact happi-
2:24f   ness during one's own lifetime. 13 And, what is more: when a
                 person is able to eat and drink and taste happiness in all his pos-
3:14-15: 1:4-11 sessions, that is always a gift of God. 14 And I perceived that
1:15   every action that God carries out occurs in eternity. To it nothing
+12:13; Prov 30:6; can be added and nothing taken away, and God has made
Sir 18:6; 42:21 humans fear him.

+1:9f; Sir 5:3   15 Whatever is occurring now, has already been there;
                     and whatever is to be, has already occurred;
                     and God will search for whatever has been chased off.

3:11 Another possible translation: "Moreover, he placed in the human mind a notion of eternity."

Overview of 3:1-15

This is the theological part of what Qoheleth, clothed as Solomon, nar-
rates. It corresponds to the announcement in 1:13-15, more precisely, in
1:13. To this extent it terminates the chiastic structure of 1:12—3:15. Yet
it begins differently from the two preceding sections of the narrative in
2:2-10 and 2:11-26. It begins with a poem. This recalls the poem at the
very beginning of the book (1:4-11). Indeed, it should recall it.

We must take into account that the book of Qoheleth is in some degree musically constructed. As in polyphonic music, various melodic themes are played at the same time. Various structures are laid on top of one another and enmeshed in one another. The theological text of 3:1-15 is apparently so important that it repeats again within itself the whole evolving form of the book up to now. Thus it stands as a sort of reiteration of all that was said up to this point. What before was stated in inner-worldly terms is now spoken in reference to God. The following schema provides an overview:

poem	1:4-11	3:2-8
reflections	1:12—2:13	3:10-11
no happiness text	2:24-26	3:12-15

For the third element, one might have described it simply as a "text dealing with joy." The motif of "joy" appears in other parts of the narrative as well. In 2:24 and 3:12 we have not only this motif but in both a very marked beginning of the sentence that leads to the themes of "happiness" and "joy." In Hebrew both texts begin with the phrase *ʾên ṭôb* ("there is no happiness"). This is found only in these two places since the beginning of the book (and later in 3:22 and 8:15).

Through this evolving form there arises a unified whole that begins not only in 1:12, but already with the poem of 1:4-11. That this is intended is further shown by the series of formulations and motifs from 1:4-11 that recur in 3:14-15, that is, right at the end. That is a clear frame for the whole text of 1:4—3:15. Details about the frame are provided below.

In general, then, 3:1-5 has a double function: it is the third section and high point of the narrative of the "king" Qoheleth about his reflective journey to the peak of his existence, and it serves as theological elaboration, providing an illumination vis-à-vis all the purely cosmological and anthropological statements that precede it.

Notes on 3:1-15

[3:1-9] This section is a sort of meditative pause in Qoheleth's otherwise concise account of his experience and reflections. It serves to universalize the experience base on which his sayings are built. This may well have seemed necessary just before the decisive theological statements. Until now the blessed existence of Solomon/Qoheleth and the equally observable counterexample—that someone painfully builds her/his world, but does not get to enjoy it—would serve to substantiate his thinking. For the logic of the thinking that would suffice, but not for its cogency, which required a literary expression. So now the fact that each human situation is determined not by those who stand within it, but from outside (in the context: clearly from God), is developed in a poem consisting of 6 + 6 + 2 (= 14) pairs of opposites.

In the first strophe, vv. 2-3 deal with beginning and ending, v. 4 with sadness and joy. In the second strophe, vv. 5-6 deal with separation and uniting, v. 7 once again with sadness and joy. Thus there is a parallel development. The short concluding strophe names the most basic procedures in human relationship, in the private and the public spheres.

The first strophe opens with two opposed sentences, beginning with the positive one; all the others begin with the negative. The second strophe has all the opposed sentences begin with the positive one; only the last pair begins in the negative. In the concluding strophe the first opposed pair begins with the positive, the second with the negative element. In the whole poem, positive sentences form the outside frame. This classification as "positive" and "negative" arises naturally in our feelings. Yet the intention of the poem is to relativize these feelings.

The very first pair of opposites refers to activities that are independent of human freedom. This sets the tone for the whole. The leading concept, which occurs in each line, is "time" (Hebrew ʿēt), behind which is the Greek *kairos* (exact point of time, critical point, occasion, propitious time).

[3:1] Verse 1 sets up the universal thesis ("everything," "everything that happens under the heavens"); 3:9 brings it together in the form of a rhetorical question. It is the answer to the question of 1:3, an answer already anticipated in 2:11.

Since everything is arranged from elsewhere, the question arises: Why should we make such an effort to change the world? Here it is formulated not as a positive conclusion, but only as a cautious rhetorical question. But the thinking goes further and this result, however right in itself, must clearly be set in a broader frame and thereby in some respects be further relativized. Toward the end of his book Qoheleth will call for energetic action (9:10; 11:4-6). How can he do this after all that precedes? 3:10-14 give the answer.

[3:5] A Jewish exegetical tradition may be correct in seeing here a veiled reference to sexual intercourse in the throwing of stones.

[3:7] Does the time "to tear" refer to the tearing of garments at the beginning of lamentation for the dead, and "to sew" represent a sign for an end of grieving?

[3:10-11] In this context, in the narrative introduction to the final step in this thought, the "business" must refer to all the various types of activity in human living that have been spread out in 3:1-9. At the same time 1:13 is cited. So what was there formulated only as a program is now to be laid out. Although the human activity in 2:17 was considered as something "evil" (*ra*ᶜ) in the reflections of the king, and the discussion of "business" in 2:23 and 26 was always given a negative tone, the background explanation given in 1:13, that the employment imposed by a god was evil (*ra*ᶜ), is not repeated. In fact, the position that now follows is totally positive, taking for granted, as it does, that human activity is always at the same time God's activity.

[3:11] In v. 11 our translation (which is to be favored over the alternative possibility in the note) starts with "All that," a phrase whose meaning is plural collective, then divides distributively through "in its time" (literally "in the single point in time of each one") and later is unified through "in all of it" (literally "in their interior"; the word "all" is repeated in the translation to bring out the meaning). The alternative translation would affirm an infinite horizon of understanding in the human spirit.

According to the words of v. 11, every action that occurs in every moment is "perfect" or "beautiful" (*yāpeh*). The basis for this is that, by God, "eternity" falls to each action's share (3:11, 14). This is to be understood in the sense of ever renewed return (3:15), through which what 1:4-11 said about the cosmos and human activity is now based on God's doing. But this cannot be grasped by human understanding ("find out," 3:11) because of our limitedness. Here, against human experience and against the analysis of this experience up to this point, "meaning" is affirmed in the light of the opening cosmology.

[3:12-15] It is not meaning and continuity of humans and for humans, but rather participation in the meaning and continuity that comes from God to the whole cosmos and hence also to human action. Nothing that accompanying time chases off is lost (3:15). To remain present in a situation that is by no means determined by oneself, but determined from without by an incomprehensible God, trusting that from God all is beautiful and real—

that surely is the "fear of God" of which 3:14 speaks: a shuddering before a God so inconceivably other, and yet so deeply implicated and close in one's own action, the "fear and trembling" of Kierkegaard. Later, 7:14 will make this more concrete.

[3:12-13] Before the concluding sentences in vv. 14-15 are heard, vv. 12-13 pick up the end of the preceding section (2:24-26). There it was stressed that the happiness possible for humans is not based on ourselves. Here in 3:12 this is recalled by way of introduction: "there is no happiness in activities" (literally "in them"—referring more likely to the activities, i.e., the theme of 3:9-11, not to humans themselves, who were last mentioned in the singular, "human"). But now the emphasis is on the affirmation that happiness is possible—in this life; and it is underlined in a somewhat padded expression that this is a gift of God. Through 3:12-13 the unit 2:24-26 is mirrored and brought to a close.

[3:14] But there is more. Out of the critically developed reflection beginning in 2:12 there remains one positive fact: happiness, if God provides it, comes in to humankind as our portion (for the word see 2:10, 21). This fact is in some degree given new illumination in the theological reflections. It is *the* "gift of God" (3:13; see 5:18). The "fear of God" of 3:14 is silence before the divine mystery, which is closed to human understanding. Can the joy given to humans perhaps be the point where this silence is overcome in an experience of divine communication? 5:17-19 will reflect further on this question.

[3:15] The concluding sentence in 3:15b may be an old familiar saying, which here is to be newly understood within the meaning of Qoheleth's theology. It closes the circle, along with 3:15a ending 1:12—3:15, with the central sentence of the opening poem in 1:9-10. Another framing link for the whole of 1:4—3:15 is the recurrence of the word "eternity" of 1:4 and 10 in 3:11 and 14.

Social Critique I

Injustice in Judgment 3:16-21

16 There is something else that I have observed under the sun:
>   in the very place of justice, there is lawlessness;
>   and in the very place of law-abiding, there is lawlessness.

17 So I thought to myself: it is God who judges both the law-abiding and the lawless. For
>   for every interest there is an appointed time,
>   and for every action in that place.

18 With regard to humans as individuals, I thought to myself, God has singled them out and (from this) they must recognize that in reality they are animals. 19 For
>   fate awaits each human,
>   and fate awaits the animals.
>   One single fate awaits both.

As these die, so the others die. Both share the same air. There is in this no advantage for the human over the animal. Both are a breath. 20 They both pass to one place.
>   They both come alive out of the dust;
>   and both return to the dust.

21 Who perceives if the air of a human really goes upward, while the air of an animal descends down to earth?

3:16-22: 8:12-15
5:7

3:1

+2:14; Ps 49:13, 21
6:6
3:20-21: 12:7;
Gen 2:7; 3:19;
Ps 103:14; 104:29;
146:4; Job 34:14f
Sir 17:1; 40:11;
Wis 2:2f

3:19 Literally: "For each man is fate, and animals too are fate." Or: "For each human is chance, and animals too are chance."

3:21 Read with all the ancient translations: *hā ʿōlâ* and *hăyōredet*. The MT has: "Who knows the air of a human, which goes up upward, and the air of animals, which descends down to earth?" MT has circumvented the prickly question of the text by making a small change in its pronunciation (article in place of interrogative particle). But then the text makes no sense in its context.

Overview of 3:16—6:10

This section, which is interrupted by the central pericope of the book—the religious critique—can be called "Social Critique." In contrast with the preceding analysis, which began with the most favorable human opportunities, this section describes and critically reflects on the evil in society, and above all on the difference between poor and rich.

Now will be unfolded what was introduced by a single example (2:18-23) in the book's major development of its argument, and whose complex character was also indicated in the poetic passage of 3:2-8. Just as one sees through the royal fiction, one becomes aware of a naive identification up till now with the mentality of a Jewish aristocracy fascinated by wealth and enjoyment, which had made its way up only by oppressing and exploiting the general population. With what unquestioning assurance had Qoheleth/Solomon in 2:7 provided himself with masses of slaves, and in 2:8 with concubines. But now the next section shows that that was only a dialectic step. We had to begin with the highest possible opportunities for happiness. Only when these had shown their dark side should the harder reality be fully introduced. Thus everything Qoheleth has reported to us as his past insight is now relativized. But not in the sense that the readers should relativize the existential philosophical insights we have gained, just because they were gained from a one-sided, and false, social perspective.

The new section of the book, unlike contemporary social critiques, does not aim at any change in society through reform of its structures. At most in 5:8 the Ptolemaic system of renting out the royal lands is preferred to the traditional system of free farmers on their own soil, which had long ago degenerated into a system of large holdings with masses of men and women in bondage, day laborers, and slaves. Moreover, it seems that, in the book, there is no awareness that society is something that humans themselves make. But rather the critical observations about the social sphere allow Qoheleth to repeat now one aspect, now another, of his already completed basic arguments, to clarify them and deepen them. Much that was only mentioned is now more broadly developed. After the demanding mental effort of the coherent logic of 2:3—3:15, the reader is not again asked to undertake any protracted reasoning.

One theme follows loosely upon another, and only from 5:12 on are the examples bound strongly together again through a continuing argument. The prose of first-person narrative is retained, but the structure of each unit is variable and here and there other stylistic forms occur. The beginning of the new section is recognized not only by the change in

theme, but also by the new introduction formula, which breaks off from
the narrative flow: "There is something else that I have observed under
the sun" (3:16; *wĕ'ôd* found only here in Qoheleth). The end of the section in 6:10 is inferred from the fact that 6:11-12 is clearly an introduction to a new section. One can dispute whether the line should be already
drawn between 6:9 and 6:10. Then it would correspond exactly to the
middle of the book, if one counts verses. But the "stronger" one of whom
6:10 speaks will be death, which was the topic above; and the forward
references to the section of the book that lies ahead begin only in 6:11.
For the limits of the pericope in the middle, see the overview of 4:17—
5:6 (pp. 74–76).

If we leave the religious critique in the middle pericope aside,
observations of form alone yield ten units, of which six precede and four
follow the middle pericope:

   1. 3:16-21   Injustice in judgment
   2. 3:22   *Happiness as the sole portion for humans*
   3. 4:1-3   Exploitation
   4. 4:4-6   Rivalry
   5. 4:7-12   One who is alone
   6. 4:13-16   The fickleness of popular favor
          [4:17—5:6]
   7. 5:7-11   The power of office and greed
   8. 5:12-16   Bankruptcy
   9. 5:17-19   *Happiness and God*
  10. 6:1-10   Living without joy

The second and second-to-last unit—texts symmetric in the structure—
fall somewhat outside the continuous theme. They deal with happiness.

In contrast with 1:12—3:15, where Qoheleth relates essentially (at
least in the sense of the fiction) personal life experiences and analyzes
them philosophically, he now tells us about observations he has made on
the fate of others here and there, and around the whole world. This is
expressed in the phrase, repeated again and again in this part of the book,
that Qoheleth had "observed" (3:16, 22; 4:1, 4, 7, 15; 5:12, 17; 6:1). In
5:7 he says to the reader—retaining the "you" address of the previous
unit—"When you observe." This expression "I observed" opens units.
Only in 4:15 does it occur in the middle of a unit. That can be explained
by the fact that the story of the example there had first to come to the
decisive point before one could speak of observing. There is usually

added (or otherwise stands close by) the phrase that the observation is "under the sun," or also within the sphere of "the earth," "in the province." In the previous sections of the book, as in the following, the expression "I observed" does not occur nearly as frequently or as regularly. So it may serve as the structural signal in this section of the book, as did the closing "breath" formula in 2:12—3:15. The word "breath" occurs ten times in the whole section 3:16—6:10, including the religious critique. But in this section it is used freely, and does not always occur in a conclusion. Obviously, it no longer has a structural function.

Not all the units of the social critique, presenting themselves in this form, are negative. The second, and the second-to-last, as mentioned above, speak of the good, and do not include the word "breath." But they too are introduced as "observations" and therefore should be considered as separate units.

Notes on 3:16-21

[3:16] In v. 16a Qoheleth is certainly not introducing a familiar proverb that he would like to "observe" or test out. The location "under the sun" makes that interpretation unlikely, as this phrase will appear again and again in what follows, at the beginning of units without any proverb style.

The proverblike doublet in v. 16b is not about a judgment in the next world, since this is "under the sun." Otherwise the development from v. 18 on would be unintelligible. This brings the reader to understand, at least upon reflection, that in v. 16 injustice in judgment means the condemnation of innocent people to death. Qoheleth presents this shocking fact, in a striking doublet, as his own personal observation.

The formulation in two affirmations sharpens its thrust also by the fact that the only variation consists in the introduction of the other member of the traditional pair, "justice and law-abiding."

Apart from the mere arbitrariness of justice, especially in regard to the poor, which may have been widespread, in the case of Ptolemaic Judea we must also take into account the overlapping and confusion of different legal systems. A native-born tax collector, independently of any traditional and local justice, but on the basis of right-of-conquest (the land was conquered, rebellions had arisen and been put down), could have local magistrates condemned, if they had failed to deliver extortionary tributes because they felt responsible for the people.

[3:17] Immediately after the theological considerations of 3:1-15, Qoheleth builds on his new observation by pointing out first that God is a participant, even in a horrible event like that. As proof he cites in v. 17 the general principle of 3:1 in a more contextualized form. One cannot exclude God from an event in the world, just on the grounds that something immoral is happening. Translators and commentators have almost always escaped this hard statement by interpreting v. 17 as God's judgment on human injustice in judging, whether this happen later on, or even in the next world. God would himself judge once again both just and unjust judges, when, in a time to be determined by him, this would occur "in that place," that is, before God. As 5:5 and 7:17 show, Qoheleth most certainly does hold that God gets angry and judges. But here the reference to the preceding theological reasoning, which is cited, makes this understanding of v. 17 impossible. Perhaps the second epilogist wanted to understand the text in this way; cf. 12:14, and earlier, 11:9.

The phrase "in that place" at the end of v. 17 means the places where humans render judgment (v. 16).

[3:18] Parallel to the role of God in connection with corrupt judicial practice, v. 18 turns to the victims of this practice (individual humans). It is clear from v. 17 that they are not only victims of human injustice, but at the same time God excludes them from the number of the living. From the experience of their own annihilating death they must learn that, as humans, they are also only animals. The Hebrew has a play on words: *šehem-běhēmâ hēmmâ lāhem;* the translation ("that in reality they are animals") cannot successfully render this phrase.

[3:19-21] In vv. 19-21 Qoheleth further develops this comparison between humans and animals, a frequent topos of Epicureans, popular philosophers, and satirists. The key word is "fate" (cf. 2:14-15, where, in a less perilous context, the educated and the fool were compared). Verse 21 expresses skepticism concerning an otherwise unknown theory about the difference between human and animal death, which Qoheleth himself will work with even poetically in a modified form (12:7). It may have been developed from Genesis 2–3.

But there was also to be read at that time a sentence in Euripides that whatever sprouts from the earth returns to the earth in death, whereas whatever proceeds from the *aithēr* (heavenly sphere) ascends to it again.[1] This could be a formulation of a Platonizing belief in the immortality of the soul, found perhaps in the popular culture that Qoheleth addressed.

---

[1] See Euripides, *The Suppliants* 532ff., in *Euripides with English Translation*, vol. 3, trans. Arthur S. Way, LCL (New York: Putnam, 1930).

For in v. 22 he will pick up—by sheer association—the positive conclusions and observations of the "anthropological" section, namely that in this world and before death, happiness is possible, as joy that humans reap from what they do. Cf. 2:10, where this was stated positively, but not yet exclusively. 2:24 and 3:12-13 were making another point.

Happiness As the Sole Portion for Humans 3:22

+2:10; +6:12   22 So I have observed that there is no happiness except insofar as one finds joy in one's activity. That is one's portion. Who could enable a person to taste something that will happen only afterward?

[3:22] As is shown in the clearer formulation ("under the sun") found in the similar verse 6:12, "after him"—to translate MT literally—does not mean specifically "after his death, in another world," but simply "later." However, this seems to be directed at some of Qoheleth's contemporaries whose hopes were for a "portion" that awaited them "later" beyond death.

Exploitation 4:1-3

5:7   4:1 Again, I further observed all that is carried out under the sun in order to exploit people. Just look:
        the exploited ones weep,
        and no one comforts them;
        from the hands of those who exploit them comes violence,
        and no one comforts them.
7:2; Job 3:20-23;   2 I always congratulate the dead, who have already died, and not
6:3-5; Jer 20:18   the living who must still go on living. 3 I would consider to be still happier than either the one who has not been as yet, and who has not observed the evil activity that is carried on under the sun.

[4:1] The third "observation" of the social critique section is introduced in a kind of litany style, as was the first in 3:16. It is about the exploitation, by wealthier classes, of the people settled on the land and of the handworkers living in cities. In the framework of the institution of debt slavery, the wealthy had direct control over workers and their work; or else they alone, through their monopoly status, were in a position to gather money in return for the products of the harvest and crafted wares, in sufficient quantities to meet the various demands made by the government through its ever more systematic and powerful bureaucracy. The use of violence was not at all excluded, especially in the case of debt slavery. If a family had put all its adults and children who were able to work at the disposition of a creditor, and had mortgaged all its houses, the last step in exploitation was the brutal sale of people into slavery in foreign countries, as this was practiced in the Greek system. (Cf. the situation that preceded the reforms of Nehemiah two hundred years earlier, Neh 5:1-5.) The oppression of the lower classes, according to the fourth "observation" in 4:4, is based on the fact that every transaction and business operation no less than every public service employment within the Ptolemaic system was characterized by rivalry.

[4:2-3] The exploitation begets the lamentation of the exploited (v. 1). Just as Qoheleth himself once reacted in 2:16 with a lament, there is here in v. 2 a lament disguised as its opposite, namely the praises of the dead and of those not born. These praises, found in the Old Testament in Job and Jeremiah, are unceasingly sung in Greek writers from Homer to Hegesias, a contemporary of Qoheleth and head of the Hedonist school in Alexandria. Here this turn of phrase allows Qoheleth to avoid identifying himself with the oppressed.

Rivalry 4:4-6

4 And I observed that every labor and every successful action means rivalry between people. That too is breath and an inspiration of air.

> 5 The fool folds his hands,   Prov 6:10; 24:33
> and eats his own flesh.

> 6 Better a handful with quiet
> than two handfuls with labor and an inspiration of air.   6:5; Prov 15:16;
>   16:8; 17:1

Overview of 4:4-6

The fourth "observation" in v. 4 shows that the oppressors are so entangled in the struggle of competition for the sake of success that they are just as badly off as the oppressed. Out of this, two proverbs are formulated in vv. 5-6 as closing argument for the "breath" formula. To the second at least has been added by Qoheleth the phrase "an inspiration of air" as a kind of coda.

Notes on 4:4-6

[4:5-6] Verse 5 is an astonishing saying of old-time wisdom: against all the rules, it can happen that also the unskilled and not so industrious people can have enough to eat. Verse 6 praises moderation because it saves humans from too much strain. But in this context both these sayings have the same function as the ironic praises of the dead and not born in vv. 2-3: if not veiled lamentation, then at least an expression of perplexity. For one could stay out of the system of competition and its resulting exploitation of humans by humans, and still one would have enough to eat and a lot more peace and quiet. But what you would not have in that case is "happiness," which, as full enjoyment of life, can come only through being fully wealthy.

If we do not take vv. 5-6 as precisely intending the opposite, by an ironically broken citation of current opinions (for which, after vv. 2-3, all reasons are given and which may be insinuated by the coda in v. 6), then we must tie Qoheleth, because of this text and this text alone, to those currents of popular philosophy that rejected wealth, withdrew from public life, and looked for happiness in that *hēsychia* (quiet) that is assured by modest restraint in lifestyle. Other utterances of Qoheleth about happiness do not support this.

One Who Is Alone 4:7-12

7 Again, I further observed a breath under the sun. 8 It happens that a person stands alone, and there is no second. Yes, not even a son or brother. But his possessions are limitless, and moreover his eyes are not sated by wealth. But for whom am I laboring, and why deny myself happiness? That too is a breath; it is a bad business. 9 Two are better than one, if it happens they are well rewarded by their possessions. 10 For if they fall, the one can lift up his partner. Too bad for the one who falls, with no second to help him up. 11 Moreover:
> When two sleep together, they warm one another;
> but how will one alone get warm?
12 And if someone can overpower one person,
> still two will resist him;
> and a three-ply cord
> will not soon be broken.

1:8; 5:9; Prov 27:20
2:18f; Sir 14:4

1 Kgs 1:1-14

Notes on 4:7-12

[4:7-8] The new unit begins with the same words as 4:1, except that the theme, even before it is named, is introduced as a "breath." By now "breath" has become a fixed concept. All analyses up to this point, except where they reach out into the domain of theology, have ended with this concept, so now Qoheleth can put this tag on something even before he starts. Even though, according to 2:18-19, an ultimate situation is presented in that one has to hand over one's possessions to a successor whom one cannot then control, still the situation is equally problematic for a person who cannot leave off work and world building, even though one works alone and has neither child nor family members. In 4:2-3 and 5-6, Qoheleth identified deeply with the people he spoke of. But here in v. 8 he goes even further into empathy. He formulates the critical question by shifting to direct discourse in the first person. In it one realizes also that frantic work can itself be an obstacle to happiness.

[4:9-12] After the "breath" conclusion in v. 8, Qoheleth resorts again to the tactic of 1:13—2:2, and of the previous unit 4:4-6, namely presenting a justification for the "breath" formula through concluding proverbs. Here, however, he offers a broader proverbial composition that begins with prose. It deals in favorable terms with communal sharing among humans. Everything is set in opposition (v. 9, *haššěnayim min-hāʾeḥād*) to the case of a person standing alone (v. 8, *ʾeḥād wěʾên sēnî*). The examples of vv. 10-12 focus on situations in traveling: a tired traveler stumbles (v. 10), the cold at night (v. 11), ambush (v. 12). Compare Homer, *Iliad* 10.224-26: "When two go together, one of them at least looks forward to see what is best; a man by himself, though he be careful, still has less mind in him than two, and his wits have less weight."[2]

But the beginning of the whole section in v. 9 shows that the idea of togetherness is not so much linked with the idea of friendship or even marriage. Here there is rather business cooperation in view. For the word "partner" is used, and as a condition for preferring community over being alone it is expressly indicated that one must take for granted that work and possessions would lead to "reward" or income. The "happiness" of v. 8 is undoubtedly what is meant here.

In 4:7-12 there is mirrored, probably unintentionally, the experience of individual isolation of Qoheleth's period, as the old social groupings fell apart—the cherished family and clan communities—and an ancient class-based ordering of society imposed itself. This was far more massively felt in the upper classes than among simple folk, for whom the old structures were just now breaking down.

Overview of 4:9—5:11

Why does Qoheleth take such pains here in 4:9-12, almost anticipating the style of chapters 10–11, to develop a picture opposed to what

---

[2] Richmond Lattimore, *The Iliad* (Chicago: University of Chicago Press, 1951) 224.

he described before, and that is envisioned in the way of traditional wisdom texts? It may be that he feels he has presented his analyses in very individualistic focus, especially through his royal fiction. As that is not his intent, he takes this occasion to make a small correction.

There may also be a structural reason, at this point, for the broadening of sayings that come in an almost ethical mode. In 4:13-16 there will follow a further "social critique" section; then the inserted, ethically oriented, "religious critique" central text of the book; and then the extension of the "social critique" in 5:7-8 follows and opens once again into a proverbial composition in an almost ethical mode (5:9-11). One can wonder whether the central text of 4:17—5:6 has not been fitted, far more carefully than one first thought, into a structured framework, through this purely formal concentric composition.

Ethic: sapiential	4:9-12	
Theme: governance		4:13-16
Religious behavior		4:17—5:6
Theme: governance		5:7-8
Ethic: sapiential	5:9-11	

This does not belong at the level of the real book structure, but it is a subordinate structure that supports the book structure and serves to underline the central text.

4:13-16: Sir 11:1-6

Prov 17:2

1:9-11

The Fickleness of Popular Favor 4:13-16

13 Better a poor young man who knows,
    than a king who is old but a fool—
because he no longer perceived that he should take advice.
14 The young man was freed from prison and became king, even though he had come into the world destitute, while the other already reigned. 15 But I observed that all the living who walked about under the sun sided with the next young man who arose in his place. 16 The people carry on, whoever it is that leads them. Moreover, the most recent generation will not be full of joy about him either. For that too is a breath and a spirit of air.

Overview of 4:13-16

The proverbs with which the foregoing unit ended are probably the occasion for beginning here not with the "I have observed" phrase that has become usual, but rather with a saying that is marked off from the previous sayings only by subject matter. The text moves then into narration, and only in the midst of this there comes a point where it says, "But I have observed" (v. 15).

With the saying in v. 13, Qoheleth probably had in mind events that originally were either historical or legendary, familiar to his readers but not available to us. The narrative intention of this atemporal and generally applicable proverb appears only after "because," when suddenly prose takes over and a narrative continues in the past tense, just as though what preceded had been narrative.

Generally vv. 13-16 deal with three leaders: the old king who was dislodged, the young man who was released from prison in order to dislodge him, and "the next young man" who "arose" in the place of the second. The rapidity of this description of a sequence of three leaders, and the gently ironic presentation of the approval "of all the living who walked about under the sun," underline stylistically what this is about: the fickleness of popular favor and the insecurity at the top of the political ladder.

In passing, there is here introduced for the first time a form that will dominate later in the deconstruction section of the book: a traditional proverb placed at the beginning of a unit is refuted at the end.

Religious Critique

4:17—5:2: Jas 1:19

Hearing, Sacrificing, and Speaking at Worship 4:17—5:2

17 Watch your step
 when you go to the house of God.
 Enter in order to listen,
 and not, as the fools do, in order to deliver a sacrifice.
 They do not even perceive
 how to do evil.

1 Sam 15:22;
Prov 15:7f; Hos 6:6

5:1 Don't be too fast with your mouth;
 and in your heart don't burn
 to make a speech in the presence of God.
 2 God is in heaven,
 you are on the earth,
 so let your words be few.

Dreams come with a multiplicity of business;
 and the voice of a fool with a multiplicity of words.

10:14; Prov 10:19

4:17 Another possible translation: "in order to give a sacrificial banquet."

Overview of 4:17—5:6

In 4:17 there is suddenly introduced the second person singular imperative form of a wisdom admonition, and it predominates until 5:6. Equally abrupt is the introduction of a new subject matter: it deals with religious behavior, and it warns rather than commands. It is not the behavior of sinners or lawbreakers that is criticized, but rather that of the *kĕsîlîm*, the uneducated, the "fools" (4:17; 5:2, 3). It seems to be concerned with religious busybodies, with the typical goings-on of popular piety, where the line is not drawn between upper and lower class, but rather within Qoheleth's own circle of well-off readers (see 4:17 alternative translation; 5:2).

74

Concretely, 4:17 deals with the practice of sacrifice (either the numerous sacrifices, or sacrificial celebrations that unfolded in festive banquets, which Qoheleth contrasts with "listening"); 5:1 deals with wordy prayers (which in ancient cultures were always spoken aloud and publicly); 5:3-4 deals with the tendency to make a vow apropos of every need (and then later not to fulfill it); 5:5 deals with the abuse of rites of atonement for unintentional sins (*šĕgāgâ,* "inadvertence"; see the law in Num 15:22-31) through which one could easily hide from oneself the fact that real guilt had occurred, involving divine punishment (v. 5 seems to consider as a new and serious sin this declaration that only an "oversight" had been made). Possibly in 5:2 and 6 under the key words "dreams" and "words" there is a hidden reference to another element of popular religion, speech: oracles, ecstatic utterances, and prophecies. It might even include a reference to apocalyptic, which was then at its beginnings.

Qoheleth's positive advice about religious behavior is prepared in 5:1b: "God is in heaven, you are on earth"—a withdrawal, therefore, from an attitude toward God that has lost its distance from the recognition of the Wholly Other, or is in some way collegial with God. It comes to expression in the very last words of 5:6, which is a strikingly abrupt line, following upon a line that the reader must feel has been stretched to an unusual length by the insertion of "puffs of breath" in the middle of a normal word sequence: "then fear God." With this, we are suddenly drawn back into the center of Qoheleth's thought (see 3:14).

This fear of God is not limited to special religious activities, or able to be expressed through them alone. Rather, when life is freed from inauthenticity, it is the hidden essence of each moment of normal living. Whoever possesses it, moreover, is one who "knows." With him every activity is bathed in the light of freedom. Only such a person would be even capable of "doing evil." Fools, if they constantly, and properly, undertake atonement rituals for "oversights," would certainly not be in a position to do evil (4:17b, which takes its meaning from 5:5).

In general, this is an unanswerable criticism of religiosity that is still perfectly valid in our day. It is not a solemn repudiation of any external form of religious worship, but only an instruction to behave well within this normal sphere of human existence. What alone matters is that the fear of God, which transcends any particular ritual act, must not be damaged. Thus this critique of religion in the central piece of the book (see the Introduction) according to its subject matter is akin to the last section, "Ethic." Both offer advice, not to draw us away from the world, but rather to root us more deeply in what is normal, albeit in the light of a wholly new knowledge.

The structure of the admonitory unit is artful. The sequence of 6 + 6 + 2 lines is repeated.

4:17	6 lines	sacrifices	linkwords A
5:1	6 lines	prayers	linkwords B
5:2	2 lines	PROVERBLIKE SAYING ON DREAMS, 1	
5:3-4	6 lines	swearing oaths	linkwords A
5:5	6 lines	rites of inadvertence	linkwords B
5:6	2 lines	PROVERBLIKE SAYING ON DREAMS, 2	

Each group of six corresponds to a theme (see above). The subject matter of 4:17 corresponds chiastically to that of 5:5, as does 5:1 and 5:3-4. Repeating linkwords, on the other hand, unite the groups of six in parallel correspondence: 4:17 to 5:3-4, and 5:1 to 5:5. The two groups of two offer proverblike foundations, each for the preceding twelve lines, on the one hand; and, on the other hand, they are related directly to one another: the second builds on the first, and at least 5:6 could suggest, without becoming too clear about it, that Qoheleth wanted to speak even further of visions and prophecies. Taken together, the admonitory unit contains 2 x 14 = 28 = 4 x 7 lines (see 3:2-8).

Notes on 4:17—5:2

[4:17] "The house of God" must refer to the temple in Jerusalem. "Enter" then means walking through the temple courts.

5:3-6: Prov 20:25;
/ Sir 18:22f;
Num 30:3;
Deut 23:22

Vows 5:3-6

3 When you make a vow to God,
don't delay in carrying it out.
God takes no interest in a fool:
Whatever you vow, carry it out.
4 It is better to vow nothing,
than to vow and not carry it out.

5 Don't permit your mouth
to bring your flesh down into sin.
Never declare before the messenger:
"It was an oversight."
Why should God rage about what you are saying,
and destroy the actions of your hands?

+Num 15:25; Lev 4f
Num 15:22-31;
35:9-25

6 Rather, when dreams multiply, and puffs of breath and
      endless words,
then fear God.   +12:13

Notes on 5:3-6

[5:3-4] Menander offers the advice, "When you swear an oath to God, do
not believe that he forgets it" (*Sententia* 347). But here Qoheleth is also
supported by a text from his own tradition (Deut 23:22-24). He follows it
verbatim in part. He changes only one thing: he transfers to v. 5 the statement of Deuteronomy that God would consider a vow made and not fulfilled to be a sin involving a guilt worthy of death, and thereby he
connects it to the unallowable *šegāgâ* declaration. In place of this statement he introduces the following, regarding the vow: "God takes no
interest in a fool." In a theological context, this cannot be dealing with the
notion that a fool cannot find approval among humans. God is the subject
of this remark. Whoever does not fill a vow forfeits divine approval. It is
to be noted here that Qoheleth once again characterizes the sinner as a
fool.

[5:5] "Sin" is probably meant in the sense of punishment for sin that God
inflicts, because the mouth tries to talk its way out of it simply by declaring past behavior to be "oversight" or inadvertence. It affects the "flesh,"
the body. Sickness is probably meant, if not death. Verse 5 shows that
Qoheleth fully expects that God can act out of anger and punish (see
7:16-17). He also holds that God's action is always perfect (3:11). What
he denies throughout the book is only that humans can perceive the logic
of divine action, and thereby get a handhold to manipulate their own
future.

    "The messenger" is generally taken to refer to the priest who col-
lects the declarations of *šegāgâ,* "oversight," along with the corresponding sacrificial offerings.

Social Critique II

The Power of Office and Greed 5:7-11

3:16; 4:1;
Exod 23:6-9;
Mic 7:3

7 When you observe that the poor in the province are destitute, and justice and law-abiding thwarted, don't be surprised when interests work this way:

> one higher up covers for another,
> and others even higher up are behind both of them.

8 But still it profits the land when a king takes care of its fields.

1:8; 4:8

9 One who loves money
> never has his fill of money;
> and anyone who loves luxuries
> never has sufficient income—that too is a breath.

Prov 19:6; 6:2

10 When prosperity increases,
> the numbers of those who eat it increase.
> What benefit remains for the owner?

6:9

> His eyes can only look.

11 Sweet is the sleep of the worker,
> whether he has a little to eat or a lot.
> The full belly of the wealthy man

+2:23; 5:16

> does not let him rest in sleep.

Overview of 5:7—6:10

The second half of the social critique is characterized primarily by the theme of possession and wealth. The theme comes into full expression in 5:12—6:10, the second largest prose section of the book. In 5:7-11 it is prepared beforehand, but these verses serve at the same time as a frame for the central text, the critique of religion, 4:17—5:6. For this reason they also take up other themes, especially governance, and include a rather substantial text segment in the form of proverbs. The second-to-last section, 5:17-19, with its positive affirmation about happiness, corresponds symmetrically to the second unit in the social critique section, 3:22; and it contains, as though incidentally, the theological statement that is perhaps the most important in the whole book.

Overview of 5:7-11

The new theme—exploitation of the poor by the powerful—is connected back to the textual unit that preceded the "religious critique" insertion by its links to the themes of 3:16-22 (injustice in judgment) and 4:1-6 (exploitation). Whereas Qoheleth previously "observed," in v. 7 he now speaks to the readers about their own observations. With the motif of "king" in v. 8, he picks up by association a thread from the last bit before the insertion (4:13-16). The mention of "poor" in v. 7 also recalls the young man in 4:14 "who had come naked into the world." So it is clear that the "social critique" section resumes after it broke off in 4:17. It is about injustice and exploitation from above. But it is not only the powerful who are above. The wealthy are also there. The powerful are rich. So this unit provides a transition to what then follows, all of which is based on the opposition "poor—rich."

Notes on 5:7-11

[5:7-8] With respect to form, 5:7 continues the second person singular address of 4:17—5:6, which suggests that 4:17—5:6 was not secondarily inserted but originally intended to be there. The character of vv. 7-8 as continuation is further indicated in that the location in Jerusalem ("house of God," 4:17) is now broadened to Judea (called "province" in 5:7 in an Alexandrian perspective).

The problem of official authority is presented under two aspects: patronage (vv. 7b-8) and, later on, greed (v. 9). Qoheleth's statement about patronage does not lead to a "breath" conclusion, but rather to a concrete evaluation of two agricultural policies: the ancient one and the one gradually imposed under the Ptolemaic bureaucracy. At most Qoheleth's position may be suggested by the use of the word *ḥēpeṣ* (here translated "interests"), recalling the same word in v. 3, where it expresses what God favors and protects.

[5:7] Why can nothing be done to combat this exploitation and this system of justice favoring certain classes? Verse 7 explains that there is almost inevitably going to be a basic complicity among all of those on whom simple folk in the countryside are dependent. Beside the village authorities, there are the officials of the Jewish temple authority and a bureaucracy reporting directly to the king. All three incessantly exercise various forms of control and collect tributes. The raising of taxes, either in the Greek system or the new Egyptian system, was contracted out to the rich local families who worked with the bureaucracy. Moreover, military and administrative emissaries traveled through the land with royal commissions and were permitted to approach private businesses as well. The interests of all the above were united in one aim: to take from the inhabitants as much as they could as rapidly as possible. Within this statewide system of exploitation, small farmers also carried on a struggle for independence against the owners of large tracts of land and the city merchants. The elites often played the role both of private competitors and at the same time of official tax collectors. Regarding the system of debt slavery, see the commentary to 4:1-6.

[5:8] Within this complex system of mutual protection, which could never be penetrated from below, v. 8 still sees a possibility of choice between two agricultural policies, one of which seems preferable. The ancient system in Israel of free farmers on their own land had been transforming itself, through the gradual enslavement of more and more individuals, into a system of relatively few large estates, whose city-dwelling owners cultivated them with the help of landless day laborers, of workers bonded in various degrees, and of full slaves; on the other hand the Ptolemaic authority was trying to impose in Judea, as elsewhere, a policy of turning as much of the cultivated land as possible into royal land (Greek *gē basilikē*). Royal land was cultivated by landless but free (*sōmata laika eleuthera*) contractual tenants (*geōrgoi basilikoi*), who could not be enslaved by private persons. A portion of the royal land was leased to high officials (*gē en aphesei*), who leased it further under similar conditions. The leaseholders were eventually obliged to contribute up to two-thirds of their harvest. Did Qoheleth see in this system more secure foundations than in the old, completely denatured system where eventually the enslavement of most of the people seemed inevitable?

Although certainty is not within reach, another possible interpretation must be considered. It is striking that v. 8 speaks of "profit" not for the farmers or the poor, but rather for the "land." We can see in 10:16-17 that Qoheleth easily links the king and the prosperity of the land. But still the shift of perspective here is surprising. Is a voice other than Qoheleth's introduced here? Would someone else be cited here, or would he himself present this familiar answer as an objection?

The problem is the total lack of an introductory phrase, or interrogatory particle, or other verbal indicator of such a change of voice. We are not yet in the stylistic realm of chaps. 7–8 where we would rightly expect such citation, on the basis of the introduction in 6:11-12. So we cannot be certain.

The objection would point out that, despite all the exploitation of the poor and all the injustice, still the policy of converting farmland into royal land is a positive development. In v. 9 Qoheleth then would interfere with this technical bureaucratic exchange by proposing a familiar proverb about the insatiable character of greed. This exposes the underlying motives and energies.

[5:9-11] As to literary form, v. 9 begins a series of sayings, though v. 9 at its end has the breath formula. A chiastic structure of linkwords marks the unity of the whole:

5:9	"fill"
5:10	"eat"
5:11a	"eat"
5:11b	"full"

Each of the sayings plays within itself with word correspondences. The "breath" formula lends shape to the series: v. 9 describes the insatiability of greed; vv. 10-11 provide grounds for this assertion. Throughout, motifs and linkwords are set up that will recur in the immediately following prose analysis in 5:12—6:10, for example, "to eat" and "to fill," the two structuring words of 5:9-11. Qoheleth 5:9-11 does, more or less, for 5:12—6:10 what 1:13—2:2 does for 2:3—3:15.

There are remarkably few parallels in Israel's sayings tradition for 5:9-11. On the other hand, behind "those who love money" we can recognize the Greek *philargyros*, and behind "if they love luxuries" the *philoploutos*, of the Cynics.

[5:9] In any case, in v. 9 there is a formal proverb concerning greed, possibly a generally familiar one. It suggests simply that the leading classes, who are being discussed here, are greedy, and it then concludes with the "breath" formula, justifying this by a series of sayings that follow in familiar form. That is a new development of thinking, reaching to v. 11.

[5:11] Verse 11b may refer to overeating or to the anxieties attendant upon many possessions (see 2:33).

5:12—6:10: 2:20-23

Bankruptcy 5:12-16

+2:17
12 Something evil happens, something like a disease, that I have observed under the sun: gathered wealth, placed for its owner in the bank, is lost in bankruptcy.
13 Through bad business dealings, this wealth was lost. The owner had fathered a son, but now there is nothing in his

Job 1:21
accounts. 14 As he came from his mother's womb—naked, as he came, so must he once again begin his life. There is nothing which he can ever draw from his possessions, which he had deposited in his account. 15 So this too is something evil, something like a disease. Just as he once came, so must he begin his life again. And what profit does he gain laboring for air? 16 Even more:
   All of his days he will eat in darkness,

+2:23
   with constant vexation, and illness and depression.

Overview of 5:12—6:10

The following overview deals with the three remaining units of the social critique section. They belong very closely together. They form the second extended, coherent, prose text of the book. It can be considered a broad working out of 2:20-23. Both the content and some aspects of form show that this case is taken precisely from the anthropological section. "It happens" in 2:21 corresponds to 5:12 and 6:1 (otherwise only 8:14; 10:5). "Evil," which often occurs and weighs upon humankind in 2:17, 21, recurs then in 5:12, 15 (otherwise only 8:6; 10:5). In style, 5:12—6:10 is similar to the prose of 2:3—3:15, and here too, similarly, the first-person narrative recedes toward the end.

The text is organized by three "observations." The case of 2:20-23 (a person tires himself out, and someone else enjoys the fruit of all this labor, even while the first one is still alive) is twice worked out, in 5:12-16 and 6:1-2, with diverse connections each time: in one, the rich man is in the foreground, and everything is taken from him while he must work through his debts; the second time, another enjoys the fruits.

The second description of the case in 6:1-2 is theologically formulated, and it seems that for this reason it is preceded in 5:17-19 by a positive presentation of God's relation to human happiness. This inserted "observation" picks up the thought from 2:24 and 3:10-15 and develops it further. 5:17-19 and 6:1-2 are shaped by their formulation as image and counterimage.

The case of 6:1-2 is further developed in progressive and varied secondary cases, vv. 3-5 and 6-9, reaching to the fantastic in vv. 6-9.

Even when one enjoys a large family and long life (vv. 3-5), or even if a fantastically long life were allowed, still we are talking about a wise but poor person, and so all of that is no use unless some good fortune occurs. The two diverse examples are linked with a praise of being stillborn, vv. 3-5 (see the ironic praise in 4:2-3), and with a further discussion of death (vv. 7-8). A proverb concludes the last case (v. 9), and a saying the whole unit (v. 10).

In 5:12—6:10 we have the exact counterpart to the image of the successful drive to prosperity depicted in 2:3-10, which portrayed a serious possibility for the head of a rich Jewish family, even if it was raised to royal fantasy. Here the contrary is presented, and one does not have the power to choose between the two for oneself. Therefore Qoheleth must extend his reflection on unhappiness toward the certitude of death just as he did earlier in his reflection on happiness.

Despite 5:7-8, the social-critical reflections are all thoroughly in keeping with the theological-anthropological reflections of 1:12—3:15. The individual thoughts are not easily deciphered. As the basic concepts have already been coherently laid out earlier in the book, Qoheleth allows himself to be led by separate proverbs to one or other allusion or further illumination. To understand his pattern of speech, we need to recall how musicians work through variations on themes.

Notes on 5:12-16

[**5:12-15**] Our translation follows the hypothesis that this section employs technical phrases from business and banking—phrases that are sometimes not known from other sources, but whose meaning can be surmised. The telltale clue that leads to this view is the technical meaning of *běyādô*, which occurs twice here. Normally it means "in his hand"; but we have a Hebrew text from the same historical period that uses the phrase in a business context with the technical meaning "on his account."

[**5:12**] After 2:17-21, "evil" can replace "breath," giving it a sharper profile. Here, and in 5:15-16 and 6:2, this is further extended by the key word "disease." When a rich man did not succeed in enjoying life, this was deemed to be a "disease" by the Cynics as well.

[**5:13**] The son is named in the description of the case, so as to indicate how normal the situation of this wealthy man is. That future appeared to be assured. In the rest of the verse, and in vv. 14-16, nothing further is said about the son, but only about the wealthy man himself. The son motif remains important, because it will be picked up in 6:3 and further modified.

[5:14] Verse 14 extends the concluding observation of v. 13 by suggesting a concrete scenario. In contrast with Job 1:21, his "going" is not to be seen as his death. What we see is that his creditors who press their demands hold back all his possessions, even the clothes on his back.

[5:15-16] Verses 15-16 use motifs from vv. 12 and 14 to summarize everything, but one new and pointed element is added to the summary—a favorite figure of ancient rhetoric. We now are focused on the subsequent life of the impoverished rich man. He has to pay his debts, probably in debtors' servitude, if he is not sold into slavery. The text, with aristocratic readers in mind, will no more than suggest this. Verse 16 begins with the same words as 2:23. Moreover, the word "vexation" in this closing verse recalls the same word in the closing verse 2:23.

Happiness and God 5:17-19

+2:10 17 Consider what I have observed—perfect happiness consists in this: to eat and drink and taste happiness through all one's possessions for which one has labored under the sun during the few days of life that God has given one. For that is one's portion.

6:2 18 Moreover, always, when God has given a person wealth and holdings, and has empowered one to consume them and maintain one's portion and find joy in one's possessions, the real divine gift consists in this, 19 that one will not much remember how few are the days of one's life, because God continuously answers through the joy in one's heart.

5:17 Literally: "the happiness that is beautiful," or "the good fortune that is full."

[5:17] "The perfect good." Greek phrases lie behind this expression: the lyrical *kalon philon* and the phrase *agathon hoti kalon* that replaced it in more elevated philosophical speech following Plato. In the context of Qoheleth's book, however, something different is primarily intended. The word "good," which up to now has been used alone and usually translated as "happiness" in context (2:1, 3, 24; 3:12-13, 22), is here linked with the word for "beautiful" or "perfect," which has occurred only once before this, where it refers to God's action (3:11). If something is now to be characterized as "the perfect good," it is thereby suggested that in this "good" the divine action, along with that "perfection" which is hidden from humans (3:11), might be experienced. Through this phrase, v. 17 begins with theological dimensions, even if the word "God" does not occur until near the end, and there almost casually.

[5:18-19] Verses 18-19 move forward, whereas v. 17 had merely recapitulated the contents of 2:24; 3:12-13, 22. What is new is that the good, insofar as it is a gift of God, is now described phenomenologically. When someone is happy, the thought of death—precisely the point to which Qoheleth wants to bring his readers—retreats from their consciousness. It becomes rare. The good is, therefore, an ecstasy that unites consciousness around one point. What point? Here, unfortunately, we run into almost insuperable difficulties of interpretation. Many translations read: "because God leads them to focus on the joy in their heart." This implies that the best part of joy is not the psychological phenomenon of joy itself (which may be no more than a physical pleasure, an explicable sense of bodily well-being), but rather the forgetting of self that an active person experiences while striving in quest of happiness. The translation we have adopted ("because God continuously answers through the joy in one's heart") would imply that the ecstasy of the good is given within the psychic phenomenon of "joy" itself—insofar as this is also a divine "answer," something like "revelation." This would mean that in joy itself that specific reality is grasped, in a nonconceptual way, which human reflection can reach only through the thought of death, and through the reasoning that leads to an inference of the perfection of God's action. Granted the supreme value that the book of Qoheleth places on the thought of death and on the gift of joy, one is tempted to prefer this second interpretation. For then the ecstasy of the good does not serve to repress the terror that is entailed in thinking, but rather transforms it by absorbing it into itself. In joy, then, the conclusion of right thinking— namely the perfection and the eternity of divine action within all events— is directly communicated as revelation.

Living without Joy 6:1-10

6:1 There happens one evil which I have observed under the sun, and it weighs heavily on individuals. 2 God gives someone so much

+2:17; 5:12; 8:6
5:18

wealth, holdings, and honor that he lacks nothing of whatever his
5:10; Lk 12:20   gullet desires, but God does not empower him to eat it, because a
Sir 14:4   stranger eats it. That is a breath and it is an evil disease.

3 If someone has a hundred children and lives many years, so that
his life is really long, and if his prosperity cannot serve to sate his
4:3; Job 3:10-16;   gullet, even if no grave were awaiting him, I say: a stillborn child is
Jer 20:17   better than that person. 4 Because:

As a breath it came,
into darkness it passes,
in darkness its name remains covered.

4:6   5 Moreover, it has never observed or perceived the sun. So it is at
rest, whereas he is not. 6 And if he lives two thousand years, but
3:20   does not taste happiness, do not both pass to one and the same
1:7f; Isa 5:14;   place? 7 All human labor is for the jaws of death, and its gullet is
Hab 2:5; Prov 27:20;   never satisfied. 8 What profit for the one who knows over the fool;
30:16   or what for the poor, however perceptive, in making his way
to 6:8: 2:13-15; 9:15   among the living?

5:10; 11:9   9 Better to have something before your eyes
than to have a hungry gullet.
That too is a breath and an inspiration of air.

1:9; 3:14f; Gen 1;   10 Whatever has occurred
Amos 3:2; Jer 1:5   it was already called by name.
It was also perceived
that each one is only human,
Job 9   and that he cannot fight
Wis 12:12   with someone stronger than himself.

6:3 Another possible translation: "to fill his gullet, and in the end he receives no burial."
6:6 Another possible translation: "a thousand times a thousand years."
6:7 Literally: "All human labor is for one's mouth, and yet one's gullet is never satisfied."

Notes on 6:1-10

[6:2] "Stranger": it may be that what is meant is no more than someone who is not a member of one's family; but usually *nokrî* refers to a foreigner. Non-Jews from neighboring areas, such as Ammonites in the east or Idumeans in the south (some of whom were Phoenician in origin) had also settled in Judah. Moreover, Greeks from the highest social classes in Alexandria had rights to fees in the province of Syria and Phoenicia, to which Judah also belonged, and these they later received as private property. So the Jews of Jerusalem's leading circles were no longer exclusively among themselves.

[6:3-5] See Euripides: "If someone strikes it rich, and has amassed a fortune, but never tries these good thing in his home, I would never say that he is fortunate."[1]

[6:6-9] In this unreal case of one who just lives too long, the starting point is expressed only in v. 8, where it is added on as a general affirmation: it is presupposed that the subject is a person who is cultivated but poor. If you exclude this wrinkle, then the case is resolved at the end of 6:6, and the theme of death's inevitability is attached, and in its perspective the educated and the uneducated are compared, recalling 2:13-15. This theme, by association, would be seized by a related theme in the same v. 8: the educated person who is also poor (see below on 9:15-16).

[6:6] The motif of "going" from 5:14-15, which there was considered as something within living, is now taken up again as leaving this life, dying. The "one place" is the region of the dead. The translation here makes this explicit in v. 7, where the Hebrew had only "*his* mouth." The closing question in v. 6 has the rhythm of a lament for the dead.

[6:7] As the theme of good fortune has been treated throughout, from its beginning in 5:9-11, in images of hunger—eating—being filled, Qoheleth here describes death as the one who is the really ravenous, who really eats, who is really never sated.

[6:9] The feeling of closure results from the proverb form. Its meaning can be understood in very diverse ways, so that there reigns a distinct ambiguity. In the mentality of traditional wisdom, it can mean that a bird in the hand is worth two in the bush. Since it stands in the context of death as a hungering gullet, however, one might also understand: better living than being dead (see especially 9:4). On the other hand, 5:10 had given a negative tilt to seeing with one's eyes. Should we then understand that even if we cannot but see the good fortune of others while we are laboring, this is still better than being dead?

This proverb that gave the impression of being the closure is followed by the "breath" formula, and, in a technique now becoming familiar, the definite closure to vv. 6-9 is brought in by a new saying in v. 10.

---

[1] Fragment 198 from August Nauck, ed., *Tragicorum Graecorum Fragmenta*, 2d ed., supplemented by Bruno Snell (Hildesheim: Olms, 1964).

[6:10] The passive verb forms make God the unnamed subject of what is said. "Acquire a name" in Near Eastern thought means: "come to being" (see 6:4). Should we understand, in the sense of cyclic theory, that every activity which one carries out has already been in existence before now (1:9-10; 3:14-15)? Or, in the sense of 3:1-9, does it say only that God has determined everything? In any case, limits to human existence are set for all humans. We cannot defend ourselves. Against whom? The text does not indicate who is meant by "someone more powerful." God (see Job)? Death (see what precedes)? If God is meant, see Menander §187: *mē theomachei*, "Fight not against the gods," from the lost play "The Eunuch."[2]

---

[2] *Menander: The Principal Fragments,* trans. F. G. Allison, LCL (New York: Putnam, 1930) 352–53.

Deconstruction

Introduction 6:11-12

11 There happen many words that only multiply breath. Of what profit are they to a person? 12 For who perceives what is better for a person in their lifetime, during the few living days of one's breath, which one carries out like a shadow? And who can tell anyone what will occur afterward under the sun?

7:11f; 7:1-18; 8:17

7:15; 9:9
8:13; 1 Chr 29:15;
Ps 39:6f; Job 14:1f
3:22; 7:14; 8:7; 9:3;
10:14

Overview of 6:11—9:6

Whereas the pericope 3:16—6:10 had laid out the basic themes of the book's beginning on a wider basis of experience, and explored some of its aspects, there now ensues a debate with the very different intellectual universe of Qoheleth's readers and hearers. So this section may be described as an ideological critique. Every society constructs a symbolic worldview that constitutes its superstructure, and an educational system to communicate it to new generations so as to make them competent in living. For a bourgeois society, for example, this was classical education, and for some parts of our world it has been socialist humanism. In Israel, or at least for the upper class of Judah to which Qoheleth addressed himself, it was a body of teaching called "wisdom." This was communicated above all, though not exclusively, through sayings (cf. the Book of Proverbs). These dealt with the most varied human situations, but most of all they circled around wealth, human rights, and situations at court.

The praise of knowledge and education played a major role in assuring the self-legitimation of the educational establishment and in motivating students. Great emphasis was given to the quality of one's speaking and self-control, the power of good repute, the destructive influence of gossip and calumny. One thesis, presenting itself as the experience of many generations, carried a lot of weight: education and knowledge assured a long life (it was clear that one must die at some point; but dying too soon was to be feared). Moreover, there was the underlying principle that whatever one does turns back upon oneself in a consistent deed-consequence relationship (in this regard, divine retribution was only one special mechanism): good behavior brings good fortune, and bad behavior brings ill. This view of reality seemed plausible, and prepared a young person for life ahead, in a world of equally entitled farmers and of small towns with a manageable style of life, where mutual support was the basic rule within the clan and the local community. In Qoheleth's unpredictable world such a view no longer sufficed, and this led Qoheleth, who was open to decisive influences from Greek culture, to design a new view of reality. He could, however, gain acceptance for the new only after he had explicitly deconstructed the old. For this reason, the next section of the book is set up with the following pattern: a typical element of traditional teaching, usually in the form of a familiar proverb, is cited and then deconstructed.

After the tension of the long prose essay, 5:12—6:10, the text resumes in a loose form. Qoheleth simply comments on proverbs by means of other proverbs. Then, first briefly in 7:10, but ever more broadly from 7:13 on, the answers come in prose as well. In the final unit (beginning in 8:16) we have only prose, and the presupposed proverb is indicated only by suggestion (8:17). The criticism of traditional teaching is naturally based, for the most part, on arguments developed earlier in the book. However, there is no lack of new observations and reflections, as in 7:25ff.

It may be that the dialogical character of the unit has led to its increased use of "you" as a form of address. The pericope begins with a kind of motto in 6:11-12. In 7:23-25 there is, as it were, a brief pause with a glance backward and a glance forward. From 8:5 on the text offers once again a coherent development of argument. One can differ about the closure of the section (after 8:16? or after 9:6? cf. also the discussion of 9:7—12:7); nevertheless, 8:16—9:6 does seem to be still another dispute with traditional teaching.

One can identify ten units in all, in each of which a typical thesis of the wisdom tradition is refuted. Before the first and the sixth introductions there are summaries and previews.

– 6:11-12   Introduction
1. 7:1-4   Fame
2. 7:5-7   Knowledge

It is clear that the whole section breaks cleanly into two halves, though the halves differ as to length. In the translation, a cited tradition and its critique are taken to form a unit. A dash is used to separate the two.

For Qoheleth's approach in this section, and again in the final ethical section of the book, it is important to note that he is not trying to determine what is always and everywhere good for humankind as such, but rather what is good for each individual in his or her life. A similar sharpening of focus is repeated in 7:15 and 9:9. State ideologies of a Marxist type can attempt to sweep away this kind of focused argumentation, but their answers to the questions of the individual people are never satisfactory.

As for content, rhetorical questions are used to express skepticism about the capacity of traditional wisdom education to analyze reality and to provide reliable insights about human behavior.

Compare Pindar, "Olympian Odes" 7.24: "But countless are the snares that hang around the minds of men, and there is no means of finding out what is best for a man to light on, not only now, but also in the end."[1]

Notes on 6:11-12

[6:11-12] Verses 11-12 form an introduction to 7:1—9:6.

[6:11] "Words," that is, sayings as they are cited and deconstructed in 7:1ff. "What profit" is picked up in 7:11-12.

[6:12] "Better" refers to the common proverb form "Better A than B (because . . .)," which in 7:1-14 plays the role of marking traditional

---

[1] *The Odes of Pindar,* trans. John Sandys, LCL (New York: Putnam, 1930) 73.

sayings and opposed sayings. In 7:1-10 there are seven such sayings, in v. 11 there follows an eighth with a more complex structure.

Individual word groups refer ahead to texts as far as chap. 8, as above in 1:12—2:2; 2:12; 5:9-13, that is, "days of breath" in 7:14-15; "will occur" in 8:7; "like a shadow" in 8:13; "under the sun" in 8:14; "carry out . . . under the sun" in 8:16-17 (see 9:3).

Fame 7:1-4

Prov 22:1;
Sir 41:11-13

7:2-3: 11:9—12:7

Sir 7:36;
╱ 2 Cor 7:10f

7:1 Better a name esteemed than scented creams—
     and the day one dies than the day one was born;
  2 better go to a hall of grieving
     than go to a festive hall.
     Since this is the end of all humans,
     let those who still live lay it to heart.
  3 Better vexation than laughter,
     for by a troubled face are hearts headed aright.
  4 The heart of those who know is in a hall of grieving,
     the heart of fools in a hall of joy.

Overview of 7:1-4

A very subtle use of language is at play here. When traditional wisdom texts had lined up proverbs one after the other in apparently casual or playful order, still it often linked them together, and not only through association of contents, but also at the level of repetition of words, assonances, rhymes, and so on. Such a linked series of proverbs is to be seen up to v. 12. In v. 14 the key word "afterward" closes a first circle back to 6:12.

Verse 2 and vv. 3-4, for example, are constructed in parallel: "Better . . . . Better. . . ." At the same time, the outer lines form, through a chiastic correspondence of key words ("hall of grieving," "festive hall" / "hall of grieving," "hall of joy"), a frame containing the inner lines, each of which ends with "heart." Then, almost imperceptibly, v. 4 introduces a pair of concepts ("one who knows" / "fool") that cannot help but invite the proverb in v. 5.

Many other strands of this linguistic web can be seen even in the English translation. As a result, the form of language here arouses the expectation of a lovely old-fashioned tapestry of sayings. But precisely this expectation is systematically upset at the level of content. In a variety of sequences the traditional statements are proven to be off-center, meaningless, and false, either by subtle shifts of perspective or by direct oppositions.

This realistic tearing up of conventional knowledge is, moreover, reflected also in the form of discourse. Gradually bits of prose appear within the chain of proverbs. From about v. 13 on, prose overgrows the linking of proverbs. From v. 14 it uses a typical prosaic phrase ("I have observed") to take over explicitly the form of discourse.

Notes on 7:1-4

[7:1] The saying cited in v. 1a (in Hebrew a heavy play on words: *ṭôb šēm miššemen ṭôb*) may well have comforted a poor man who suffered from the realization that feasting was beyond his reach, since he had no money even for the ornaments and perfumed oils appropriate to festivity. He possessed a higher good: his good reputation ("name"), which he had won even without money, purely through his virtue and his personal role in the community. The same saying may also have found application in the same milieu when, at a burial, spices were lacking for anointing the corpse—his reputation ("name") was more important. Here Qoheleth's witty continuation is casually tacked on in v. 1b, without even repeating the word "better," as though it were an obvious conclusion. He takes the saying literally. With razor-sharp wit he cuts to the insight that this supposedly great benefit of reputation accrues at death, whereas it is totally absent at birth. Thence comes v. 1b.

[7:2-4] The following three verses then draw further conclusions. They proceed on several levels. Nothing is said that cannot be drawn out of v. 1a. But no one would have formulated such conclusions before now. It is all both irony and derision. The pretty saying is dragged on *ad absurdum*. Yet a deeper seriousness remains because, as though by accident, Qoheleth has ended up in the middle of one of his major themes: life must be understood from the perspective of death.

Moreover, the reader of the book up to this point knows full well that Qoheleth has no desire to fix lines of grief on our face, but rather to move us to joy in the face of death. Everything is both right and false at the same time. But Qoheleth wants this dialectical play to go further. He has already placed in v. 4 the hooks upon which he can hang his next wisdom citation.

Knowledge 7:5-7

5 It is better to listen to the criticism of one who knows,   Prov 13:1; 15:32
   than to become fans of the song of fools.

6 For, like the crackling of thorns under the pot,
   so is the laughter of a fool.—
But that too is a breath, because:

Exod 23:8;
Deut 16:19

7 Blackmail dulls the wit of the wise
   and a bribe leads understanding astray.

7:5b Another possible translation: "than that someone listens when the ignorant serenade him."

Notes on 7:5-7

[7:5-6] The previous unit can be understood merely as a criticism of folk wisdom. The worldwide learning of the cultured classes would be something else. Verses 5-6 cite a proverb that contains the self-praise of the culture of higher society. It betrays a consciousness of class. Doubtless the original readers could detect this on the basis of the rather exaggerated pomposity of its wordplay (*šîr*, "song"—*sîrîm*, "thorns"—*sîr*, "pot"—*kĕsîl*, "fool"). Qoheleth raises an explicit objection to this by the "breath" phrase.

[7:7] The objection is then argued in v. 7 by another proverb, possibly a traditional saying. Ordinary people came in contact with the cultured precisely as representatives of an authority or as ministers of the law. In this contact they also experienced the results of blackmail and of bribes. The susceptibility of the cultured classes to such pressure lays bare their moralizing maxim and shows it as ideology. Here Qoheleth does not react only on the level of theory, but he examines praxis as well.

Caution and Conservatism 7:8-10

1 Kgs 20:11
Prov 24:20
Prov 22:24

1:11; 7:23

8 Better the outcome of anything than its beginning;
   better an air of caution than an air of impatience.
9 Don't be blown about in an air of your vexation;
   For vexation is at home in the belly of fools.—
10 Do not ask:
   How came it about that earlier times
   were better than present times?
For such a question will not make you appear knowledgeable.

Notes on 7:8-10

[7:8-9] The citation in 7:8-9 is recognizable as such by its form. This has most to do with the sounds of words, and cannot be heard in English translation. Verses 8-9 offer, as content, a central theme of the educational tradition in the ancient Near East. The type of situation is behavior at court, or in the presence of exalted patrons. As it is a mistake to count one's chickens before they hatch (v. 8a), it is a mistake to show one's weapons too early. The ideal is a cautious person, biding one's time, controlling oneself, only at the end seizing the initiative at the right moment (v. 8b). One must remain aware of the general group dynamics, and not allow oneself to be controlled by personal feelings (v. 9). Qoheleth then reacts once again in an unexpected manner. He asks: What kind of person is developed by this kind of education? His study seemingly has shown him that it will be a conservative person, one who lauds time past and has contempt for the present. If the conjectures developed in the Introduction concerning Qoheleth are on target, he may have had in mind many of his colleagues from the temple school in Jerusalem; he had broken out of that circle. His reaction here is against this type of person. He does this, in any case, in a very elegant manner, making the transition almost imperceptibly.

[7:10] He merely extends the proverb a bit further in v. 10. The warning in v. 9 was connected back to v. 8b. Now he adds a warning, parallel in form to v. 9, which chiastically links back to v. 8a. Verse 8a could be literally translated: "The later of a thing is better than its beginning." Therefore, Qoheleth argues, how can we say that earlier times were better? The tradition has been taken at its word, and confronted with an offspring that contradicts it. An educated person demonstrates, by the very textbooks of his education, that he is uneducated. Right away the reader of this v. 10, which incidentally has broken out of meter and surrounds the saying by free prose, recalls 1:11. There it was suggested how one might get the idea that new things happen, that is, that the times deteriorate. 7:24 will touch on the same topic.

Qoheleth is coming gradually to the end of the skirmish: he begins to refer back to his earlier argumentation. This he will do quite openly when it comes to the following citation.

Is Knowledge a Means to a Long Life? 7:11-18

11 Knowledge is as good as an inheritance, and is even more profitable for those who see the sun;	Prov 16:16
12 for one who shelters in the shadow of knowledge, is also in the shadow of money; but the profit from perception is that knowledge keeps its owner alive.—	Prov 3:1-2, 13-18
13 But note the actions of God: for: Who can make straight what he has bent?	3:14 1:15

+3:11; +6:12; **14** On a happy day, take part in the happiness; and on a bad day,
Job 2:10; Sir 11:14   take note: God has made the latter just as he made the former, so
                          that humans can find out nothing about what comes afterward.
3:16f; 8:14; 9:1f;   **15** In my days of breath I have observed both cases: it happens
Ps 73:12-14;   that a law-abiding person, despite the law-abiding, comes to a bad
Job 21:7   end; it happens that a lawless person, despite the lawlessness,
to 7:16f: ⁄ Sir 7:5-8;   has a long life. **16** Don't be altogether too law-abiding and don't
32:4   profit too much from what you know: why should you destroy your-
2:15; Lk 18:9-14   self? **17** Don't be utterly lawless, or become totally ignorant: why
3:2; Prov 10:27   should you die before it is time? **18** It is best you hold on to the
                          one without losing your grip on the other. A God-fearer, in any
+12:13   case, will escape both dangers.

Notes on 7:11-18

[7:11-12] The fourth citation, picking up the word "knowledge," is created with the following complicated structure:

11a	"A is as good as B
11b	or rather even better."
12a	Supporting argument for 11a
12b	Supporting argument for 11b

Verses 11-12 are so filled with Qoheleth's favorite words that, one might
think, only the sentence "In the shadow of knowledge, in the shadow of
money" existed before Qoheleth. Qoheleth may have then extended it,
but in such a manner as to express the self—self-understanding of the
traditional education system. The horizon of its known universe offered
the same protection ("shadow") as inherited wealth. But what is more, on
this basis, a person can live in keeping with this vital wisdom in such a
way that the law of deed-consequence relationship will not bring on an
early death, but allow one to enjoy a full lifetime.

   With the expression "see the sun" in the sense of "to live," a Home-
ric phrase that had become commonplace in Greek poetry is here
stamped upon the Hebrew language. In Hebrew one would expect the
expression "to see the light." As we will see, it is probably not unintentional that the introduction of the teaching of deed-consequence relationship occurs in a text formulated by Qoheleth himself. His colleagues,
whose belief in this regard he will present, would probably have included
God in their formulation of it. Without saying it in so many words, he
here denies them the right to do so.

[7:13-14] The cited saying is first brought into question by reference to
earlier reasoning. Twice we are told to take "note," and twice God's

96

action is mentioned (in the Hebrew the same root is used for "actions" and "has made"). The reference is to the saying in 1:15 and the theological reasoning in 3:11-14. That this ends in 3:14 with the motif of the "fear of God" implicitly extends the reference to 7:18. What is remarkable about this radical questioning of the whole world perspective of wisdom is that now, against a teaching that is consciously formulated in inner-worldly terms, Qoheleth himself "theologically" takes to the field. In the name of God's freedom and unlimited power, he puts in question a way of thinking that claims to comprehend reality. Since all human activity is at the same time a divine activity beyond human ken, no future event can be calculated, especially not the time after one's own death. We can do no more than accept each moment, just as it is given us by God. In v. 14, for the first time in the book, what in 3:14 was called the "fear of God" is concretely defined: to allow oneself to fall into the happiness offered us, but also to know that God is at work in misfortune, and therefore to accept it.

Greek lyric poetry offers the same advice, but not with the same theological refinement and motive. For example the seventh-century B.C.E. lyricist Archilochos wrote: "not over-proud in victory, nor in defeat oppressed. In your rejoicing let your joy, in hardship your despairs be tempered: understand the pattern shaping men's affairs."[2]

[7:15] The theology is given a foundation in experience, which, at least in individual cases, shows the exact opposite of the affirmed law of deed-consequence relationship. That theory was valid in the closed and simple world of farms and small towns in the past. Moreover, even in the third century it may still often have made sense, insofar as change does not come to everything at the same time as society evolves. But it did not always ring true, because the far more obtrusive and very different Hellenistic international society undermined its presuppositions on all sides. So the attitudes and expectations regarding the future implied by this theory often did not pan out, and this led to a collapse of their plausibility among those who were alert.

In formulating the opposed thesis, Qoheleth introduces here, where he is dealing not only with theory but also with praxis, a new pair of concepts. Beside "those who know"—"fool" there appear ṣaddîq—rāšāʿ, translated here "law-abiding" and "lawless." The pairing of these words arises in some contexts such as a court of law. However, it had long since been adopted to characterize the relation of persons to the divine order.

---

[2] §128 in M. L. West, ed., *Greek Lyric Poetry* (New York: Oxford Univ. Press, 1993) 11.

Both the King James and Douai versions translate "just" and "wicked," and the NRSV has "righteous" and "wicked." Cf. also 8:5, where we have not *ṣaddîq*, but *šōmēr miṣwâ*, literally "one who cares for the commandment."

[7:16-17] In a fictive admonition, Qoheleth presents the situation ironically. From his experience he concludes in v. 15 that whoever holds on to the law ruins him- or herself; but whoever fails to hold on to it dies prematurely: this on the basis of the traditional wisdom theory. With the same logic, simply in reverse, the opposite naturally could also be proven. The thought is playful but the message serious and subtly formulated. All who remain true exclusively to the old ways, and so interiorize its worldview that they cannot go beyond it, will be overwhelmed by fears that leave them paralyzed and speechless when it turns out that the world is different. On the other hand, all who, in the face of social change and its concomitant reduction of plausibility, believe that their actions are now free from any obligation and their thoughts no longer obliged to hold to any worldview will in any case stumble and fall apart. Here one might think immediately of God's punishment. See the commentary to 5:5. Qoheleth could not describe all this in the categories of a sociology of knowledge. But he had observed what these mean. What can one do, then, in such a situation of radical change?

[7:18] To hold on to one bit of advice (that of v. 16), and not let the other go (that of v. 17)—this does not mean either paradoxical action or an often cited "golden mean," but rather something like a sociological eclecticism, which alone is adapted to a situation where various social systems and worldviews are mixed together at the same time. A concrete, historical human being does not live according to an eternal and unchangeable moral law but rather according to an ethic qualified by concrete relationships, which can be replaced by another. In this case, during the period of transition some areas may develop where ethical guidance is lacking, whereas in some others the former ethic still holds true, and in still others a new ethic has taken hold. To handle this correctly requires the eclecticism of v. 18a. But what determines the choice? Qoheleth says: the fear of God (v. 18b). What can carry it off then is precisely that way of understanding the world in an ultimate perspective that he has worked out, and that way of decision-making in each instance based on what has just taken place in view of the ultimate reality (cf. the acceptance of the moment in v. 14). That does not mean that this situation ethics should be something enduring and normal. Qoheleth himself, at the end of his book, will begin to develop a new concrete wisdom ethic. But in the transitional situation, which is the context of his thought, it alone makes sense.

Does Knowledge Yield Protection? 7:19-22

19 For one who knows, knowledge is a protection more powerful

than the ten rulers

who have dominated the city.—

9:16; Prov 21:22; 24:5

20 And yet there has never been a human on earth who was so law-abiding that he did what was right, without ever sinning. 21 And don't listen to everything people say. For you will never hear some-one under you speak critically of you, 22 and yet you clearly per-ceive that you have often spoken critically of others.

1 Kgs 8:46; Ps 14:3; Job 15:14-16; Rom1:8–3:20; 5:12; 1 John 1:8

Notes on 7:19-22

[7:19-22] "The city" may be Jerusalem. It is true that before 175 B.C.E. Jerusalem was not, strictly speaking, a polis. It is possible, however, that at some point earlier, in imitation of the polity of a proper polis, there were *deka protōi* (ten first men) at the head of the *gerousia*, whose power had subsequently become legendary. Or else, perhaps, that system of government well known from other cities has become proverbial in Jerusalem, precisely because it did not exist there.

In the context the citation represents traditional wisdom. Qoheleth reacts by denying that the law-abiding (which he here makes equivalent to the educated or knowledgeable) are ever completely such. Those who believe it are deluding themselves. More precisely, it is the delusion con-cerning the truth of what dependents say to the person they depend on. Basically he here, once again, uncovers an area in which circumstances have shifted without being noticed. A huge household with many slaves, dependents, clients, and possibly a whole hierarchy of social levels is an obstacle to openness. But the change is not noticed, and individuals continue to act as though they were living in the old-style united family where trust reigned and everybody really knew everybody else.

Knowledge: Traditional and Inductive 7:23-25

23 In all ways I tried having knowledge. I said: I will study to become learned. But knowledge remained distant for me.

24 Distant whatever has occurred,
    and deep in the depths—
    who could ever find it?

1:9, 11; +3:11; 7:10

‖ 1:17; 8:16
7:27, 29
8:8, 10, 14; 10:13
25 So I turned, that is, my mind turned me, around. I wanted to perceive through exploration and search out what that knowledge is
which is reckoned from specific observations. Moreover, I wanted
to perceive whether lawlessness was connected with a lack of
learning and ignorance with delusion.

Overview of 7:23—8:1a

This unit, introductory to the second half of the deconstruction section
(sixth within a series of ten) is built in a more complicated manner than
the others. Verses 23-25, in reference to all that precedes, are both a recall
and a summation, and in v. 25 also an announcement of what is to come,
in the habitual allusive style that we have seen in 1:12—2:2; 2:12; 5:9-11;
6:11-12. At the same time vv. 23-25a present the problem that will be
treated throughout 7:23—8:1a: whether inductive knowledge, based on
experience and observation, might possibly be set up differently and prove
more successful than the traditional wisdom inheritance, based on learning proverbs. On the basis of a concrete test case, the advantage of an
inductive approach is shown (vv. 27-28), and yet at the same time it
becomes clear that humans will abuse it (v. 29). The test case is drawn
from a traditional proverb concerning women (v. 26), which constitutes
the citation from tradition that is usually addressed in the context. Thus the
text deals concretely with the theme "women" at the same time. The several levels of the text do not make it simple, and so we can understand why
v. 27 explicitly takes its distance, and Qoheleth, the "leader of the assembly," is recalled as speaker, and why, at the end, 8:1a expressly draws
attention to the difficulty of the text. The unit picks up a problem that
came to the fore in Greek education after the separation of empirical
knowledge and philosophy. However, it is not pursued further in this book.

Notes on 7:23-25

[7:23] The "two ways" refer to the two methods specifically indicated in
v. 23 and v. 25: studying the tradition, and acquiring knowledge through
observation. Since 7:1 the two ways have constantly been paired—and in
that sense this refers back. In 7:23—8:1a the comparison is carried out in
an especially self-reflective manner, and in that sense it refers forward.
"Distant" means out of reach. Traditional knowledge—as has already
been established—is not real knowledge.

[7:24] Verse 24 is not simply a proverbial confirmation, but rather it gives
the grounds for v. 23. For this is not about the unreachableness of knowl-

edge as wisdom tried to mediate it (above all a life knowledge enabling one to control the future), but rather the unreachableness ("distant" and "deep") of the past. That is the reason—we should add—why the experiential bases for the inherited proverbial wisdom can never be checked. On this repeating topic, see especially 3:11; 7:10; 8:16-17. Only that knowledge is meaningful which rests on what now can be checked. The point is addressed now in v. 25a.

[7:25] Verse 25 is a repetition of 1:17, extending and clarifying it, and it refers, as does 1:17, to developments that lie ahead. Decisive are the elements that have been added to what we read in 1:17:

v. 25a	*ḥešbôn*, "reckoning"	key word in 7:23—8:1
v. 25b	"lawlessness"	key word in 8:5-15

Later 8:16 will pick up v. 25a again. While v. 25b functions as an announcement and goes no further (cf. 2:12b), v. 25a leads on, with its announcement of the shift of knowledge through memorizing proverbs to inductive knowledge, to the concrete development that begins with the introduction of a proverb in v. 26. The idea of an inner connection between ignorance and illusion is not recalled anywhere else in Qoheleth. Possibly it was blowing in the wind from the Stoa: *pantes aphrones mainousin*, "the unwise are all mad."[3]

Knowledge: Traditional and Inductive 7:26—8:1a

26 Again and again I find the claim that womankind is stronger than death. Because: (Song 8:6f; Prov 2:16-19; 5:2-6; 6:24-35)
> She is a ring of siege towers,
> and her heart a net,
> her arms are ropes.
> One blessed in the eyes of God can escape from her; (2:26; Prov 22:14; Sir 26:23)
> one whose life has failed is taken by her.

27 But look at what, in observation after observation, I have found out, said Qoheleth, until I eventually found the final reckoning; (1:2; 12:8)
28 or, more precisely, how I constantly searched and found nothing:
> Among a thousand I could find one human only; (Sir 6:6)
> but the one I found, among them all, was not a woman.

---

[3] Diogenes Laertius, *Lives of Eminent Philosophers*, vol. 7, trans. R. D. Hicks, LCL (Cambridge: Harvard Univ. Press, 1950) 124.

29 Look at the one thing I found out:
    God made human beings straightforward,
    but they have gone searching for all sorts of reckonings.

2:14; Prov 16:13f 8:1a Who then is the one who knows? Who perceives the sense of a
    proverb?

7:29 "reckonings": the underlying word (*hiššĕbōnôt*) has also another meaning: "siege machines."

8:1a Read with Aquila, Symmachus (LXX): *mî kōh ḥākām*: MT: "Who acts like a wise man? Like one who perceives the sense of a proverb / the explanation of a (difficult) thing?" If one follows the MT, the two questions form the beginning of the following section.

Notes on 7:26—8:1a

[7:26] The saying about women is presented first in indirect discourse, and then, from "because" on, in direct discourse. Qoheleth "finds" this saying. "To find" is one of the motifs that the text plays upon from v. 24 through v. 29; another is the contrasted word, "to search." The original proverb would have consisted only of the first four lines. It would have been comparable to Song 8:6, a proverb of astonishment at the power of love and the mystery of being able to bring new life into the world. The continuation that we read in the last two lines has, of course, changed everything. Now it is a saying typical of male culture. This is the type of thing one says when a classmate from the old school, a member of a sport team, or a military buddy is going to get married. And it gets a laugh. Such antiwoman talk could readily be spread from the special male youth culture of the ancient Greek world. Semonides, at the end of his poem "On Women," had similarly used the image of a rope: "Yes, this [i.e., woman] is the greatest plague that Zeus has made, and he has bound us to them with a fetter which cannot be broken."[4]

The word at the beginning of the proverb *(mar),* here translated "strong," now, because of the continuation, secondarily reactivates also its other possible meaning, "bitter." It is difficult to determine whether Qoheleth found this saying already in this mutated form, or he himself formulated an interpretive addition, in order to take a first step toward discrediting it. But the actual dispute begins only in v. 27.

[7:27-28] Qoheleth takes the first line of the proverb naively at its word: if women were more powerful than death, then women should not die. However, experience refutes this: Qoheleth makes out that he has exam-

---

[4] Hugh Lloyd-Jones, *Females of the Species: Semonides on Women* (Park Ridge, N.J.: Noyes, 1975) 54.

ined the life history of one thousand persons, and not one woman was still alive beyond a certain time. It may well seem to us that such a refutation of a profound and age-long experience is unworthy and cheap. But it is completely possible that Qoheleth consciously presents himself as being this naive. The saying touches on his central theme, death. The saying plays on it, mystifying it. That is not serious and it serves only to spread a clouded image that obstructs our view of reality, and behind which the circumstances of a bygone age can live on. Anyone who realizes that a woman exists no differently in view of death than a man, and in no way shares in some numinous glamour of death, gives women back to themselves.

[7:29] The inductive way to knowledge has proven its worth in a concrete example. Is it, therefore, to be recommended in all situations? New dangers show their faces. The words have already picked them up, and Qoheleth plays with the two meanings of the plural *ḥiššĕbōnôt,* "account" or "reckoning," and also "siege towers" (i.e., the highest technical achievements of the military industry of that era). The proverb had said that the woman was a "ring of siege towers." How innocent! The new way of knowledge has made an end of such death metaphors. But, against the will of God as creator, it has been used by humans to introduce real untimely death ever more powerfully into his creation. Archimedes, for example, was a contemporary of Qoheleth, had a residence in Alexandria as well, and maintained his connections with it. He was the inventor of the marine propeller and of many apparatuses based on windlasses, pulleys, and levers. He died in 212 B.C.E., in a war.

Being Counselor of a King 8:1b-4

8:1b The knowledge of a man makes his face radiant,   Sir 13:26
and his stony features soften.—
2 But I (to the contrary): Be attentive to the orders of the king,   10:4
because of the oath you swore before a god. 3 Do not withdraw
hastily from his presence, and do not insist on something if it   Prov 20:2
threatens to have an evil ending. For whatever he finds interesting
he will carry out. 4 Since behind the word of the king there is
power, who can ask him: What are you doing?

Notes on 8:1b-4

[8:1b] The construction of war machines took place in the milieu of royal courts. While dreaming of the best scenarios for the future, the students of ancient wisdom, in their schools, speculated about a brilliant career at the royal court. Moreover, 8:1a can be understood to mean: "Who is a good advisor in difficult matters?" which also is a speculation for the royal court. Thus the next citation provides a proverb that places before the student's eyes the most sublime educational goal (v. 1b). Obviously it has been taken from a larger literary structure. In it, "his face" was not that of the knowing advisor, but rather that of the advice-seeking king. The phrase "radiant face" is applied, in the Old Testament, to God when he turns with favor upon humans (basic text: Num 6:25). Thus royal pleasure illuminates the king's visage, when one who knows offers him advice. Even if the readers did not know the original context of the citation, or even if the original meaning intended the wise man himself as the one whose wisdom illuminated his face, Qoheleth's reply makes clear that the saying is about an advisor at the royal court.

Even though in Alexandria only people from the very top levels of Jewish society had access to the royal court (e.g., Joseph the Tobiad), and even these were certainly not official advisors, still the temple school in Qoheleth's time must have prepared its students through many ancient proverbs for court scenarios, just as if there were still a king in Jerusalem. Qoheleth goes along with this fiction, but he is thinking about the situation in Alexandria.

[8:2-4] Qoheleth dares describe the raw truth, contrary as it is to the ideals of the school, concerning the profession of royal advisors. He clothes the description in a well-meant word of advice. The courtier must hide his view and his ideals and bend before whomever has the power. Since he has sworn himself to loyalty, this is even the way it should be. Or, could it be that the reference to a loyalty oath indicates that insubordination could entail confiscation of all goods and the death penalty? The text is, at the same time, a brutal demythologizing of Ptolemaic divine kingship. The royal splendor (shining out in names such as "Savior," "Benefactor," "Divine Revelation") is reduced to what lies behind it: naked power.

The One Who Knows and the Ignorant—Their Fate, I 8:5-12a

8:5-6: 3:1
to 8:5: Prov 19:16;
Sir 15:15; 37:12

5 One attentive to the law will have no occasion to perceive evil,
    a knowing mind perceives when the time is right.—
6 Nevertheless:
    There happens a right time for every interest,
    and:

104

	Human evil is often heavy upon a person.	2:17; 6:1

and:

7 One does not perceive what will occur,   +6:12

and:

How it will occur, who will tell that?

8 There is no human who has power over the air,   Prov 30:4
   so that he might lock up the air.

There is no power over the day of death.   9:12

There is no day off in a war.

Even a crime will not win freedom for the criminal.

9 I observed all of this while I was examining all the actions that
were being carried out under the sun, during a period when one
man was using power over another in order to bring evil upon him.

10 That is when I observed that lawless people were given burial,   +1:13
whereas others who had acted justly would come to the sanctuary   Job 21:27-34
and go away only to be soon forgotten in the city. That too is a
breath. 11 For:

Where no punishment is enacted,

evil action is soon afoot,

For this reason, there arises in the human heart a desire to do
evil. 12a For:

A sinner can do evil a hundred times   9:1

and afterward live long.

8:8 Other possible translations: "There is no escape in war" or "In war there is no negotiating";
"Lawlessness does not spare those who set it in motion."

Overview of 8:5-15

The debate is resumed against the basic wisdom theory regarding the
principle of deed-consequence relationship (cf. 7:11-18). It consists of
two citations (v. 5 and vv. 12b, 13) and two critiques of them (vv. 6-12a
and 14-15). In the first part it remains ambiguous whether we have a continuation of the theme "fate of advisors to the court," or the more encompassing theme "fate of humans in the world." God is not brought into the
picture, at least not openly (contrasting with 7:13-18). In the second citation, on the other hand, the basic wisdom theory is openly presented, and
in its religious garb. Qoheleth had had the ideology that he opposed speak
until now in a perfectly secular mode, without naming God. That does not
correspond to the image we draw from the book of Proverbs, for example. Apparently Qoheleth would not concede to his enemies the right to
involve God in what they had to say. Of God one had to speak in another
way. Only now, at the climax of the debate, does he allow them to wrap

themselves in the divine mantle. His answer in v. 14 is all the more secular: a pointing, once again, to the refutation through experience of all the old theories. Only in v. 15, when he speaks of joy, does he himself speak of God once again.

Notes on 8:5-12a

[8:5] "One who is attentive to the law" is like a resumption of v. 2; the "evil" recalls the "evil ending" to an advisory session that v. 3 considered. The citation touches on the same realm as 7:8-9. The professional courtier always says only yes, and thus maintains himself in the king's favor, until he perceives that the time is ripe for him to give the advice that furthers his own ends. But "law" could also be the "law of God": Israel's law, which frequently is so named. Beneath the sly strategy of courtly life there glimmers a world principle: obedience to the law protects one from an evil fate, and the worldly knowledge of the cultured helps them to deal successfully at the right time.

[8:6-7] Qoheleth reacts once again (as in 7:13) by offering citations from his own text that refer back to earlier argumentation: compare v. 6 with 2:17; 3:1; 6:1. The two parts of the verse, 6a and 6b, correspond chiastically to the two parts of v. 5a and 5b. Verse 7 adopts the key word "perceive" from v. 5 and asserts that humans cannot reckon the future, a theme he had developed long before, but now seizing upon a new formulation (only partially preempted in 6:12). So the citation, understood in its all-encompassing sense, has long been radically refuted, but also when applied narrowly to strategy within the royal court. Further, in v. 6a Qoheleth's self-citation recalls v. 3b, because the same Hebrew root *ḥēpeṣ* recurs (translated "interest[ing]").

[8:8] Verse 8 provides arguments for v. 7, in a block of four sayings that describe experience. The basic idea is that whatever humans cannot control, whatever is set in motion from somewhere else (finally from God), these things humans cannot foresee in advance. *Rûaḥ* is "air" or "wind," but it is also "breath." When "breath" leaves us we die (Ps 146:4). The second proverb, concerning the point of death, is a statement parallel to at least the secondary meaning of the first. The meaning of the third and fourth sayings is elusive, because we are no longer certain about the translation of some words. But they must have meant, one way or another, that death cannot be avoided, and no one can ward it off. The opacity of the future is, then, essentially the darkness surrounding the moment of our own death.

[8:9] Here Qoheleth himself reveals that there are two levels of meaning in his last explanations: his experience occurred in a society characterized by the domination of some people over others, to the detriment of the dominated ones, and yet his horizon was more universal. The complicated use of passive formulations ("the action," "was being enacted") suggests a veiled discourse about God's ruling over the world. For the key word "power," an Aramaic root is used (*šlṭ*), which was used for the titles of high officials in the province.

The concrete example that now follows took place in *the* city, in Jerusalem, the place of the sanctuary. Thus that man who "was using power over another in order to harm him" may have been the one who at that time ruled in Jerusalem. We can understand why the formulation is not more explicit. This is explicit enough. Qoheleth will come back to this man in 10:1-7. See the commentary to 9:7—12:7. Here it is clearly the one responsible for, or at least who allows, the situation that 10:10-12 alludes to rather than describes, as we can again well understand.

[8:10] Here, no doubt, reference is made to persons and events familiar to the original readers.

[8:11-12a] Apparently losing himself in the description and analysis of a society characterized by evil (3 times "do evil"; the last of the 7 occurrences of *raᶜ*, "evil" or "harm," in 8:1-15), he ends it all with a fully grounded denial of the law of deed-consequence relationship, and this now in terms of the religious category "sinner" (v. 12a). This brings into play the last citation, formulated in fully abstract theoretical terms in vv. 12b-13, and the opposed position similarly formulated in v. 14.

The One Who Knows and the Ignorant—Their Fate, II
8:12b-15

8:12b-15: 3:16-22

12b Of course I recall the saying:
      Those who fear God will prosper,
      because they fear before him;
     13 The lawless will not prosper,
         and their life, like a shadow, does not last,
         because they do not fear before God.—
  14 However, it has happened that things have been carried out upon
     the earth that are a breath:
        there are law-abiding people
        to whom things happen
        as though their action were of a lawless person;

8:12f: Ps 37:17-20; Prov 10:27

+6:12

7:15; Ps 73:2-12

Jer 12:1f

and there are lawless people
to whom things happen
as though their action were of a law-abiding person.

+2:10   From this I concluded that this too is a breath, 15 and I praised
joy: for there is no happiness for a person under the sun except to
eat and drink and be joyful, should this come to accompany a person in their labor during the days of life that God has given them
under the sun.

Notes on 8:12b-15

[8:12b-13] Here in this citation (and only here and in the second epilogue, 12:13) is the "fear of God" used, not in Qoheleth's own understanding of it, but in a sense derived from the religious worldview of
wisdom that Qoheleth is challenging, where it means the faithful obser-
vance of the rules of conduct for society that God has provided in
advance. It claims a clear causal link between the fear of God and well-
being and long life.

[8:15] This verse is to be read in the light of 7:14, where the idea occurs
in a similar position within an analogous structure of affirmation, and in
the light of 2:24-25; 3:13; 5:18, where happiness is presented as a gift of
God, otherwise beyond human reach. After the citation of vv. 12-13, the
expression "fear of God" could only sound strange and false. So
Qoheleth here, when concluding his answer to the citation, seizes on the
most unique element of his conception of "fear of God" that corresponds
to his image of the opacity of worldly events and of God's freedom, and
he celebrates it: the acceptance of joy when it is given. The word translated here "accompany" does not otherwise occur in the Qal stem. It
appears to have an original meaning of "bind," or "crown." It could be
that it intends to suggest a custom of crowning with flowers the partici-
pants in a festivity ("should this circle our head like a crown out of our
possessions during the days that God has given us under the sun").

God, Death, and the Limits of Knowledge 8:16—9:6

1:8, +13, 17; 2:23;   16-17 When I had set my mind to perceive what knowledge really is,
3:10   and to observe what business is really carried out on earth, then I
+3:11; 6:12; 7:25;   observed, as to the whole of the action of God, that even if their
11:5; Sir 18:5   eyes never close in sleep, humans cannot find out what action is
being carried out under the sun. Thus humans really labor in
search of this but find nothing. Even if one who knows claims to

perceive it, he cannot find it. 9:1 For I have thought about all this and examined it, and concluded: those who are law-abiding and knowing, their actions are nevertheless in the hands of God. Such a person never perceives whether he is loved or scorned; both possibilities are standing before him. 2 Both—for everybody. The same fate awaits the law-abiding and the lawless, the good, the pure and the impure, those who offer sacrifice and those who do not. It comes to the good as to the sinner, to those who swear oaths as to those who are cautious about oaths. 3 What is evil, in all that has been carried out under the sun, is that one and the same fate awaits all. Moreover, in humans the heart is full of evil, and their spirit is seized by delusion during their lifetime—and afterward, as they are about to join the dead, 4 which one would be exempted? For all the living, there happens to remain trust. For:

> A living dog is better than a dead lion.

5 And: The living perceive that they will die; but the dead perceive nothing at all. Moreover, they receive no further reward, because their memory has been forgotten. 6 Love, hate, and envy toward them have already disappeared. In all eternity they will never again own a portion of anything that is carried out under the sun.

9:1f: 7:15

2:24
3:8
+2:14
7:15

8:11; Gen 6:5; 8:21
+6:12

+1:11; 3:8: 4:4

+2:10

9:4 Read with *Ketib* and the pointing: *yibbāḥēr*; *Qere*: "and afterward they join the dead. Whoever is classified among all the living, they have a hope."

Overview of 8:16—9:6

The tenth unit of the ideology deconstruction section is its conclusion (cf. the forward-referring key words in 6:12; 7:25, and the recapitulation of the principle that what one does turns back upon oneself), and at the same time a conscious reformulation of the main points of the anthropology/theology section to which the deconstruction section holds a symmetrical position in the overall composition of the book (cf. 1:8-13, 17; 2:23; 3:10-11; 6:12; 7:25; 11:5; Sir 18:5). Its main key word is "perceive" (especially at the beginning in 8:16—9:1, and toward the end in 9:5). One might say that the text sets one theory of knowledge against another theory of knowledge. The citation out of Israel's cultural past, which is to be expected but is only suggested here in indirect discourse, is expressed in 8:17: the claim of theoreticians until now that they possess authentic knowledge of the whole of the world event. Qoheleth had already excluded this possibility in 3:11, and here he emphatically rejects it. Compare the sixth-century B.C.E. Greek poet Theognis: "We mortals have no knowledge, only vain belief; the gods fix everything to suit themselves."[5]

The professional zeal found among wisdom teachers, however admirable it may be (8:16-17), proves to be fruitless. It does not reach the objective that is sought by the study of the last principles of the universe: that one might really know concerning oneself whether one is loved or scorned by God (9:1). That could happen only if we could establish laws governing God's reaction to this or that human action, that is, if there were an observable deed-consequence relationship. For then one could predict God's reactions to the present situation (would it be favorable or scornful?). With this, the decisive characteristic of Qoheleth's theory of knowledge becomes clear: its profound "agnosticism."

Yet human knowledge is uniquely significant. This becomes evident when the living are compared to the dead, who cease from knowing. In 9:2-4 Qoheleth offers a summation of his former discussions about the equality of all in the face of death (cf. 2:14-17; 3:18; 6:6-10; 7:2, 28; 8:8), in that it is not better for the good than for the bad (with special reference to 8:11-12). Then, in 9:4-6, this is extended into a contrast between life and death. Superficially it appears to be concerned with the darkness surrounding death. But equally stressed is that the light in living becomes visible against the darkness. The three dominant concepts are "trust," "perceive," and "reward," which concern the personal relationship between humans. The essential discovery that constitutes us as fully human is when we realize that we are that being which is headed toward death. This is not, as a commentator suggests, gallows humor, but a recall of all that was worked out in the anthropology/theology section, the journey of the spirit in existence, in which through the "fear of God" it remains present to the ultimate mystery. At the end there occurs the key word "portion," which is denied to the dead. That word links to the text concerning "joy" that follows in 9:7. The "perception" that is truly given to humans frees them to be filled with joy before God. For this is the "share" allotted to humans (9:9).

Notes on 8:16—9:6

[8:17] This verse is very important in understanding the whole book, because it makes the action of God equivalent to the activity "that is carried on under the sun," something that was to be surmised in any case from the use of passive formulations in many other texts. What is espe-

---

[5] §§133–42 in West, ed., *Greek Lyric Poetry,* 67.

cially meant is all human activity. This then is at the same time always divine activity. Yet precisely in this dimension it is impenetrable for humans, above all when we ask about the "all" of divine activity.

[9:1] The logical structure is: first comes the thesis—that even people who seem to be in the best position, the conscientious and educated, have no control over their fate, but rather God controls it. The basis for this thesis is given: first it is observed to be universally true (for all people) that no one knows how God stands in relation to him or her. Then a conclusion is drawn: what is true for all is equally true for this group of the law-abiding and educated. The specific form of the deduction—from what is valid for all to an enclosed group—is pointed out again at the beginning of v. 2.

[9:2] There then follows a rhetorical complement of associated pairs: if in all cases it remains open how God will direct the following destiny, yet at the same time in all cases one thing is certain: the final destiny of inevitable death. The opposed groups whose lot is death are lined up according to various points of view. The categories are drawn from religion: conformity or nonconformity to the various expectations of Jewish society in regard to religion. One wonders, however, how far the negative items are understood to be individuals with deviant attitudes; or was it becoming evident that opposed groups were slowly forming and constituting themselves? Perhaps even groups among whose new mentors Qoheleth himself was numbered. The counsels regarding religion in 4:17—5:6, in any case, might well suggest that people in his circles would take a rather cautious stand regarding the offering of sacrifice and the swearing of oaths.

[9:3-4] The *Ketib* text is certainly preferable, because, regarding a later orthodoxy that believed in the punishment for evil at least in the next world, it seems to exclude this as well. The *Qere* text smooths over the complication, and can only be a "corrected" text.

[9:4] "Trust": the word *(biṭṭāḥôn)* is elsewhere found only in 2 Kgs 18:19 (= Isa 36:4), though within one of the most important OT texts dealing with "trust" (= faith in the NT sense) in Yahweh (i.e., 2 Kgs 18:19). The key word in that passage is the verb *bṭḥ,* which corresponds to the noun under discussion. Does it here really mean—as most commentators opine—no more than the hope that things can go well as long as one lives, at least from time to time? Many parallels from Greek pessimism could suggest this. Compare, for example, Euripides, *The Trojan Women* 634–35: "Death cannot be what Life is, child; the cup of Death is empty, and Life hath always hope."[6]

But even if the motif originated there, perhaps something more was intended from the Hebrew word: the possibility, which humans enjoy only before death, to lead one's life in an attitude of trust. In this case, did it mean to live in an attitude of trust only within the web of human relationships (as the consideration of love, hate, and envy in vv. 5-6 might suggest), or did it mean precisely to depend on God, even though a person does not know whether she or he is loved or scorned by God, but because we know that there is nothing which is not "a breath" aside from him, and that he always acts "perfectly" even though humans cannot perceive it (3:13)? The question is not easily answered. But, despite all his fine sense of words, whenever Qoheleth gets to the most delicate point, he always remains brief and does no more than hint. Thus "trust" is perhaps meant as a new word for "fear of God," at least for those who can read. For others it can always yield a more superficial meaning, one that also is in keeping with the thought of the author.

The sentence concerning trust is rapidly terminated with a proverb, a trick of style familiar to the reader from 1:13—2:2. In order to understand the proverb fully one must note that in the ancient Near East the dog was one of the most despised of animals, while the lion was held to be king of the beasts.

[9:5] To know that we will die is the achievement that, above all, the book of Qoheleth desires for its readers. That is the way that leads to the highest grade of insight possible to humans, which places us before mystery, and holds us in mystery. The value of such human knowledge is to be fully grasped only when profiled against what death brings: the annihilation of consciousness.

The use of the word "reward" does not, at first glance, seem to make sense. However, "reward" *(śākār)* provides a wordplay with "memory" *(zākār)*. This presupposes—probably according to the popular culture that supported the cult of the dead—a correspondence between what advantage can still accrue to the dead and what the living do in respect of the dead. They counted on some form of continuing communication. Insofar as the dead are thought about on earth, they go on receiving some force of life and consciousness in their diminished underworld existence.

---

6 Quoted from Gilbert Murray, in *The Complete Greek Drama*, ed. Whitney J. Oates and Eugene O'Neill Jr., 2 vols. (New York: Random House, 1938) 1:984.

One will take all the more thought for a dead person as he or she has done good things during their earthly life. Thus will they, in fact, be "rewarded" for their life even after death. This theory, however, leads *ad absurdum* on its own. The memory of earlier times and persons rapidly disappears among humans (cf. 2:11, 16). For this reason, Qoheleth considers the dead at the moment when their memory, which at first had continued a short while, has disappeared. Their "reward" then too is gone, for they no longer possess consciousness. Only then are they really dead. The popular theory that is presupposed here, which allows for a somewhat slow and delayed loss of consciousness, may not seem so wrong in the light of much parapsychological data. It is important to be clear that this has nothing to do with theories of an immortal soul or with hope of a divine awakening, and giving a new life, for those who are already dead. In respect to such notions, if ever they crossed his mind, Qoheleth has only the "Who knows" of 3:21. But here he sets the limits of all attempts to soften the effects of death by reference to brief remaining possibilities of postmortem communication, by drawing attention to what soon definitively occurs. The dead lose what characterizes the living, and what really constitutes consciousness, namely interpersonal communication. Over time, this is something related to the living.

[9:6] Verse 6 treats interpersonal communications as a reality that is carried out under the sun, but no longer extends to the dead. The key words that are lined up there are connected by rhyme to "their memory" (*zikrām*), and doubtless belong by content to "memory" as well: *gam ʾahăbātām, gam śinʾātām, gam qinʾātām*. Their "love," "hate," and "envy" are key words, which (through 3:8; 4:4) refer to earlier extended contexts, and in this way to the whole complexity of interpersonal dealing. When one reflects on this interpersonal life, one glimpses the limit that is called death. This leads to the fear of God, and—if my interpretation of 9:9 is correct—also to trust. Again that enables one to live properly. One can take hold of joy as the God-given lot in life, and then, when occasion arises, take powerful action. These are the decisive positions presented in the framework of the book's concluding section that follows.

Ethic

Joy and Decisiveness 9:7-10

+2:10

Prov 5:18f

↗ John 9:4

7 Go ahead, eat your bread with joy, and drink your wine with a happy heart, for God long ago determined your activity as he desired. 8 Always wear clean clothes, and care for your head with hair creams. 9 Experience life with a woman you love, all the days of your life of breath that he has given you under the sun, all your days of breath. For that is your portion of life, and of the possessions for which you labor under the sun. 10 Everything that your hand finds worth doing, do it, as long as you have the strength! For there is neither action, nor accounting, nor perception, nor knowledge in the netherworld to which you are going.

Overview of 9:7—12:8

At the end, the book leads anew into considerations of living and acting. It concludes, one might say, with an ethic. From the ethical field, religious behavior has already been dealt with in 4:17—5:6, in order to give the book a center. Here at the end of the book an ethic is developed that is directed rather at secular areas of living.

There is a problem in characterizing the beginning and the end of this ethical section. Most of the text consists of a series of sayings linked primarily by association—more or less the section 9:11—11:3. Yet this thematically elusive material appears to be held together by a framework that contains the main directives. Its opening section prepares the ground for developments in the closing section. Joy in living, the theme of the closing poem and its introduction in 11:7—12:8, was also the theme of 9:7-9—that seems to be a frame. Tenacious effort, the theme of 11:4-6, was also commanded in 9:10—that would be another, inner frame. Thus there would result a framing of the last section of the book, and it would begin following 9:6.

114

9:7-9	Frame A	Joy in living
9:10	Frame B	Tenacious effort
9:11—11:3	CORPUS	
11:4-8	Frame B	Tenacious effort
11:9—12:8	Frame A	Joy in living

Concerning the starting point of this section of the book, however, a certain confusion arises through some additional observations.

First, 9:7-9 (or even 10), analogously to 8:15 that forms a closure to 8:1-14, could be a closure to what would then be considered a unit in 8:16—9:6 (see the repetition of the key word "portion" from 9:6 in 9:9). In both cases the theme of happiness would complete a long reflection.

Reflection	8:1-14	8:16—9:6
Happiness	8:15	9:7-9(10)

This would indicate a parallel development of two units within the same section of the book. It could mean either that the deconstruction of ideology section continues to 9:10, or that the last ethics section begins already in 8:16. In any case, 8:15 remains an objective account. In contrast, 9:7-10 is a directive. One cannot be precisely clear about where 9:10 belongs in this consideration.

Second, at the end of the concluding poem dealing with joy in life, the themes of death and God emerge clearly in the foreground (12:1-7), so that once again one could argue that 9:1-6, where the theme of death is also dominant, already belongs to the outer frame of the concluding section of the book.

But as the analysis above showed there are also good reasons to consider just 8:16—9:6 as part 10 of the ideology deconstruction section. There are many links by content and key words to the preceding section—a feature that is not continued in this way from 9:7 on. What is more, the exhortation by allocution in the second person singular resumes only in 9:7. So I have decided to draw the line after 9:6. But it seems that there is not just a simple line. A problem remains.

The problem can only be solved by assuming the interweaving of a twofold structure in a single unit of the text—similar to what was to be seen at the beginning of the book (see commentary to 3:1-15). As is often to be found in polyphonic music, the limits of various parts differ according to changing points of view. The points of view change during the process of listening and reading. We should try to reconstruct the experiences of a first reader.

The readers who have come to the section from 8:16—9:10 experience this at first as a conclusion to what precedes. The impression that something new begins only in 9:11 persists for some time, especially because 9:11-12 presents itself as a dispenser of key words for many proverbs that follow. Thus 9:11-12 functions as an introduction. It is only much later that readers begin to have doubts about this impression—namely when in chaps. 11 and 12 the motifs of "tenacious effort," "joy," and "death/God" recur, and indeed in chiastic correspondence to their occurrence in 8:16—9:10. Then readers will recognize, looking back from the end, a framing of the whole final section of the book that must have already begun in 8:16.

8:16—9:6	Frame A			God / Death
9:7-9		Frame B		Joy in living
9:10			Frame C	Tenacious effort
9:11—11:3				CORPUS (9:11-12 introducing)
11:4-6			Frame C	Tenacious effort
11:7-10		Frame B		Joy in living
12:1-8	Frame A			God / Death

The readers saw correctly at the beginning and also at the end. The book had played with them. In the transition from chap. 8 to chap. 9 several structures had been woven together. It is really only for practical considerations that I drew the line in the text division after 9:6.

Also at the very end of the book the situation is somewhat more complicated than indicated until now. Examined more closely, the frame themes B (joy) and C (death) were already briefly touched on in 11:7-8, and with that the end of the structure really is attained. But then immediately these two verses are shown to be no more than a brief transition and introduction to the great closing poem. This follows as a coda to the overall structure of the concluding section. It extends the two themes broadly once more: "joy" in 11:9-10, "death" together with the theme "God" in 12:1-8.

Between the frame units, which, from 9:7 on and once again from 10:20 on, have the unmistakable character of direct admonition about what readers should do, 9:11—11:5 is made up of many forms. According to the tradition of wisdom forms one would expect to find here also the genre (*Gattung*) of direct admonition. Yet it hardly occurs: only in 10:4, 20; 11:1-2. Mostly there intervene texts that, on the basis of content or of form, we would expect to find in earlier parts of the book, rather than enclosed here between the admonitions of the frame: 9:11-12, 13-16, 17-18; 10:5-7, 12-15. So Qoheleth retains a strong continuity with the earlier parts of his book also here in his ethic.

How is this possible? First, it must be noted that for ethics the wisdom repertory of literary forms also provided genres (*Gattungen*) other than admonition, for example, sayings about what is "better" than something else (see 9:16—10:1), contrasting profiles (see 10:12-17), observations of cause and effect (see 10:10-11, 18-19; 11:4). Moreover there occur fully pre-ethical descriptions of significant situations, for example, 9:11-16; 10:2-3, 5-11, 15; 11:3. In part they recall the popular folk cunning of early wisdom. From these it becomes clear that the word "ethic" does not characterize the final section under all points of view.

It is perhaps better to say that the book of Qoheleth, after deconstructing the existing body of an earlier worldview, wants now to support the underpinnings of society by constructing at least a beginning of a new worldview. However, the worldview of a society is expressed not only by a body of advice (one should act thus or so) but also, prior to that, by definitions of reality (one *is* thus or so). Only when both are present does a common understanding of the world exist upon which a human society can function. The old wisdom also handed down both, interwoven in its teachings. For this reason Qoheleth too can sometimes speak in a purely indicative mode in this concluding section, simply setting up the world anew through description. In doing so he can latch onto his own expositions along with their forms and concepts; he can also take concrete positions rather akin to the tradition he has so sharply challenged—because the battle before now was over the final most far-reaching general theory, rather than over the detail, of the world. In the latter much remains stable through all changes in society: compare Qoh 10:6-7 with Prov 30:22-23; Qoh 10:12 with Prov 15:2; Qoh 10:18 with Prov 20:4.

If such was the intent, then this section of the book, one must say, appears short and the selection very unsystematic. There must have been some principle of selection and some guiding idea. Specific areas are totally missing, for example, family behavior or neighborliness. It could be that the old lessons were still adequate in respect of such areas. The students, whom Qoheleth addresses here, may have already been educated in the style of the old wisdom. Qoheleth would then have intended to equip them only for what specifically was new, that revolution in commercial, political, and social life with regard to which the tradition offered no illumination.

117

Those addressed here were apparently losing their way in the stress of competition from their own circles to catch up with the dominant, leading Greek circles, or perhaps simply stress arising from their ascent among the limited group of the rich and influential families. Hence already the decisive examples in the anthropological and the social-critical sections, along with their constant pointing out that all the good fortune made possible through work is useless if they then do not really get to enjoy it. This now becomes the decisive admonition. On the other hand it seems to be more a concern to avoid a misreading of the relativizing of ambition for wealth and power, when enjoyment of life is placed side by side with energetic and timely action. In contrast with most of the Greek Peripatetic philosophers, with whom he otherwise has much in common, Qoheleth does not present the undertaking to provide a cornucopia of good things and to build a wealthier world as contemptible. He does not recommend dropping out, just as he never separates body from soul.

Certainly he must help his students to come to grips with their concrete situation in society, its opportunities and its limits, beyond the perspectives of the old wisdom that presupposed vanishing or already extinct conditions. Leadership is in the hands of strangers. There is hardly any opening to the levers of power in Alexandria. For this reason there are no admonitions regarding behavior at the royal court (8:14 was not an admonition, but an ironic rejection of ways of old-time courtiers). This is perceived as from a great distance, made simple as in a fable, in 10:16-17 as decisive for the well-being or woe of the land. It is present only in the form of omnipresent intelligence services and well-paid informers, in the face of which one must be on guard (10:20).

What counts is who has "power" locally or in the province, the "boss" of 9:17 and 10:4 (*môšel*). We do not know whether the provincial governor is meant (the *stratēgos*), or the high priest, or another top official of the temple-state (e.g., there was, beside the high priest, a *prostatēs* [one who stands in front]—an office held for twenty years during the relevant period by Joseph the Tobiad who was at the same time the official in charge of farming out all the taxes of the whole province of Syria and Phoenicia). The Aramaic word *šallîṭ*, which also occurs in this context (in 10:5), is vague, at least as far as our knowledge of it goes. Since it can denote all the leading bureaucrats (Dan 3:2-3), it is translated by "official." In any case, the students needed to be prepared in advance for all possible good or bad encounters in the company of these "wielders of power." In contrast with the old wisdom, Qoheleth here sketches a rather depressing picture of the possibilities for influence that a cultured or competent person should expect. Often a very different kind of person rises to the top. Thus, while keeping an eye on influence upon the "wielder of power," one should also not neglect the advancement of one's own possessions.

The text often remains at the level of images, and makes its statement only in coded language—probably for good reason! The commentary can do no more than point out the linkages through the use of key words, and indicate possible dimensions of meaning. The five-part structure indicated is very tentative. It follows some dominant themes and the use of some introductory formulas. The sayings are so strongly linked to each other that often a different division is equally possible.

At the beginning of 9:11—11:3 there is in 9:11-12 a very compact text, partially prose and partially verse, concerning the uncertainty of the future. To it there correspond thematically the concluding verses 11:1-3. These texts are once again a kind of frame, already in the inner text. Both discuss human ignorance, misfortune, something that fails. But the beginning text in 9:11-12 also has a further function. A whole series of words and formulas from it return again in the inner sections. In some way it provides the key words for the whole text. The details will be given below.

If one wants to divide further the series of sayings in 9:13—10:20, three divisions appear: the first is centered on the chances for advancement for a young man in the province (9:13—10:7), the third on one's attitude regarding the distant royal court, which one can put into action only in terms of speaking about it—something not without danger, however (10:12-20). The intervening section in 10:8-11, if one is looking for an underlying intent, is almost impenetrable. It begins and ends by speaking about a snakebite—this motif provides the frame for this section. This may warn about political reversal, or at least suggest that one think and plan carefully before taking any action.

This triple division is given a foundation in what follows. However, one could take the middle section as part of the final section. There would then result for both sections, 9:13—10:7 and 10:8-20, exactly thirteen verses each.

Notes on 9:7-10

[9:7-9] Verses 7-9 are part of the frame. In form and content they derive from the songs about enjoying life that were sung at banquets in the ancient Near East and in classical antiquity.

The closest parallels are to be found in the words of the wine maiden of the gods in the old Babylonian Gilgamesh Epic, and in the harp songs in Egyptian burial chambers.

Gilgamesh Epic

Thou, Gilgamesh, let full be thy belly,
Make thou merry by day and by night,
Of each day make thou a feast of rejoicing,
Day and night dance thou and play!
Let thy garments be sparkling fresh,
thy head be washed; bathe thou in water.
Pay heed to the little one that holds on to thy hand,
Let thy spouse delight in thy bosom!
For this is the task of [mankind]![1]

Song of the Harper

Let thy desire flourish,
In order to let thy heart forget the beatifications [funeral] for thee.
Follow thy desire, as long as thou shalt live.
Put myrrh upon thy head and clothing of fine linen upon thee,
Being anointed with genuine marvels of the god's property.
Set an increase to thy good things;
Let not thy heart flag.[2]

For similar practices in Israel, cf. Isa 22:13. In the Greek sphere the combination of motifs had long penetrated into other genres, especially in didactic texts of popular philosophy. Qoheleth speaks here for the first time—with the exception of 7:14—to command joy, not just to tell about, reflect about, or praise it. The only concrete motifs until now, of "eating" and "drinking," are extended to others all belonging in the realm of festivity. Qoheleth is no believer in the "small joys of everyday," as many moralists would recommend. He envisions great banquets. The much discussed question of whether v. 9 deals with the wife of the addressee, or one of his wives, is not part of the topic of this text, and therefore also cannot be answered from the text. Joy should constantly be sought, and the reason is: whenever it occurs, it is God who has graciously shared it. The pleonastic insertion of the breath motif shows that this command to joy contradicts nothing of what has earlier been said in the book, but rather arises from it. That is made explicit in v. 9b.

---

[1] 10.3.5ff.; *ANET,* 90.
[2] *ANET,* 467.

[9:10] Verse 10 still belongs to the frame of the concluding section of the book. The message here, where Qoheleth treats of "action," is already aimed at youth ("as long as you have the strength"), as in the final command to joy in 11:9-10. The unit that follows is linked together with 9:10 by "perception" (= "perceive") and "knowledge."

Time and Chance 9:11-12

11 Again, I further observed under the sun that:
The race does not go to the swift,
victory in battle does not go to the powerful,
nor does bread go to the knowledgeable,
nor wealth to the clever,
nor applause to the perceptive,
since time and chance await each one.
12 Moreover, humans cannot perceive their appointed time.
Like fish who are caught in an evil net,
or birds caught in a snare,
so every person is trapped in an evil time
when suddenly it falls upon them.

9:11f: +3:1

Prov 16:9; Rom 9:16

10:12; 1 Kgs 5:18

Notes on 9:11-12

[9:11-12] In order that it become clear once more that it is not in the power of humans to achieve joy and to assure success by our own effort, the teaching of the whole book on this point is brought together here in poetic form—introduced, however, in prose and at the beginning of v. 12 interrupted by a prose observation. The key word is "time" in the sense of *kairos* (see 3:1), in one case further determined by "chance" (which can be open to the good as well as to the bad), and in the other by "evil" (which leads only in one direction). "Evil time" (already expressed in the artificial wording "evil net") does not necessarily mean immediate death. Rather, when human affairs turn sour, death foreshadows itself by early messengers. For the image of the net in v. 12, compare Homer, *Odyssey* 22.386-90:

> Think of a catch the fishermen haul in to a half-moon bay
> in a fine-meshed net from the white-caps of the sea:
> how all are poured out on the sand, in throes for the salt sea,
> twitching their cold lives away in Helios' fiery air;
> so lay the suitors heaped one on another.[3]

---

[3] *The Odyssey,* trans. Robert Fitzgerald (Garden City, N.Y.: Doubleday, 1961).

The five examples in v. 11 are really, when examined, only three: (1) the athletic competitor, (2) the military leader, and (3) the rich and powerful member of the urban aristocracy who strives to provide for his family ("bread"), to surpass that by achieving the financial growth that enables political influence ("wealth"), and this political power itself ("applause"). The three last examples are separated from the first three by the threefold repetition of "nor" (emphatic in Hebrew), and so identified as the concrete point being made.

The whole series could summarize the biographical ideal of a young Greek: success in sport as a youth, then a military career, eventually setting up a family, accumulation of wealth, public influence in the polis. We do not know whether the higher circles of third-century Jews appreciated competition in sports. Jewish soldiers, and officers as well, were a treasured element in the Hellenistic armies. But here too we must ask whether the Jerusalem nobility were involved. For the Jewish aristocracy, then, normally only the last, threefold area will have acquired importance. Wisdom upbringing aimed at it, and also the educational concerns of Qoheleth.

Here he refuses his students any guarantee of success. This stands in opposition to the usual professional self-praise of the educational industry, through which it motivates students to learn. But even if self-praise is ruled out, reflection on the later placement of students in society cannot be avoided. For this reason vv. 11-12, akin especially to the equally poetic text of 5:9-11, are also an introductory piece upon whose key words broader developments will later be fastened. The details will be indicated as they occur.

Up and Down in the Province 9:13—10:7

13 And this too I observed under the sun: an example of knowledge that I considered great: 14 There was a little city. It had few inhabitants. A great king marched against it. He surrounded it and built great siege towers against it. 15 In the city there was found to be a poor man who had knowledge. He saved the city through his knowledge. Afterward, however, no one remembered this poor man. 16 So I said:

7:19; Prov 24:5
Sir 13:22f

> Knowledge is better than power;
> however, the knowledge of a poor man is discounted,
> and his words are not listened to.

17 The cautious words of those who know are more acceptable than the shouting of a boss among fools,

18 and knowledge is better than weapons—
    but a deviant individual can subvert much happiness. Prov 21:22

10:1 Dying flies—then stench and bubbles rise
    in the creams of the perfumer;
    a small stupidity proves more potent
    than knowledge, than honor.

2 The mind of one who knows takes to the right; +2:14
    the mind of the fool takes the left;

3 but the ignorant person—whichever way he walks,
    the mind is not there,
    though he has said of everyone else: he is ignorant.

4 If the boss is up in the air against you, 8:2-4
    don't withdraw from your position;
    for calmness cautions against
    seriously deviant actions.

5 There happens an evil that I have observed under the sun—the +2:17
kind of oversight that tends to occur at the hands of an official:

6 Stupidity was placed on benches raised on high; Prov 30:22
    and wealthy people had to sit beneath them.

7 I observed slaves on horseback,
    and princes walking on the earth like slaves.

9:15: Another possible translation: "He could have saved this city through his knowledge. But no one thought about this poor person."
9:18 Literally: "an individual who does something wrong."

Overview of 9:13—10:7

Framed by two pieces in the style of a report of an observation, 9:13—10:7 deals especially with the chances an educated person has in political life, and in the ambiance of a "wielder of power," probably in the province. According to 9:13—10:7 the power of the educated person to make a mark in the realm of political power is questioned by ignorance (9:13-18), even the stupidity (10:1-3) of deciders in society, namely the "boss" (10:4) and his crowd (10:5-7). This is expressed in very coded language, and the exegesis that now follows is, in this measure, quite uncertain.

Linkwords that use formulations from 9:11-12
9:13   I observed under the sun
                   knowledge

9:15	knowledge
	knowledge
	human being
9:16	knowledge
	power
	knowledge
9:17	those who know
9:18	knowledge
10:1	knowledge
10:2	who knows
10:5	evil
	I observed under the sun
10:7	I observed

To the words for knowing correspond, of course, words for not knowing that did not occur in 9:11-12. Beside these links to 9:11-12 there are other key words that also bind the very diversified sayings of this unit with one another.

Notes on 9:13—10:7

[9:13-15] The link to the preceding is the just-named life objective: "applause" for the "one who knows," that is, political influence. A story shows the problems. The original readers will have recognized the event that is referred to. We do not know it. A number of Ptolemaic and Seleucid kings had assumed the (originally Assyrian) title *basileus megas*, "Great King." In Hebrew the word "great" forms a key word against which the contrast word is first "little" and then "poor" (also 3 times).

[9:16] The lesson that Qoheleth draws from the story is formulated as a "True . . . but" observation. It reveals a first flaw in the efficacy of the intellect: knowledge must be supported financially, otherwise it is ineffective.

[9:17-18] Verses 17-18 form a further "True . . . but" train of thought, set in motion by its predecessor. We have once again, as in the section on deconstructing ideology, a dialectical interplay with sayings. "His words are not accepted" from v. 16 provokes a contrary affirmation from tradition; but this is extended by a sentence in v. 18a that is almost identical with the "true" affirmation of v. 16. Then the "But" of v. 18b opposes by noting a second flaw in the efficacy of the intellect: felicitous society presupposes the harmonious cooperation of all; failure can occur if even one person proves false.

More is not said with articulated words. Yet the "deviant individual" may well have referred to the "boss among the ignorant" of v. 17, who may well stand for the "official" (10:5) and who is more notable for the strength of his voice than for his competence. Qoheleth does not hold back from his students their precarious future.

[10:1] This verse is a proverb offered almost as a proof for 9:18. In this sense one could take 9:17—10:1 as a literary unity. But 10:1 is more than an image parallel to 9:18. A new key word appears, "stupid/stupidity." Up to now it was about a lack of education. It was something that could be remedied. It was not stupidity. Now we are shown a further flaw in the efficacy of intellect: the limits in the intelligence of those who set the pace.

[10:2-3] Verses 2-3 clarify the distinction between a lack of education and stupidity. "Right" and "left" are symbols of good and evil. The understanding of an educated person either leads to the good, and of an ignorant person to evil, or it leads the educated to success and the ignorant to failure. There we have sensible connections. The behavior of a stupid person, on the other hand, has no kind of rational basis, neither well developed nor badly developed. A foolish person lacks insight into his or her own reality, but projects it into other people.

The unidentified subject of 10:1-3 would be the "boss" once again, or at least his group. In favor of this interpretation is that now more openly, one after the other, the themes of "boss" (v. 4) and of the circle of the officials (vv. 5-7) are taken up, and that in v. 6 the closest circle of the powerful are considered as stupidity incarnate. Thus the full understanding of vv. 1-3 becomes possible only when one reads further on. It is important (and mostly overlooked by commentators) that this is not about the "king" (in Alexandria) but about locally available high officials, who were more significant for those addressed by this book. The expression translated "boss" (which in no way refers especially to a king) in v. 4 is possibly qualified by the old saying in 9:17. The person meant is probably identical with the "official" of v. 5 (and the one "wielding power"—the same Hebrew root—in 8:9).

[10:4] Linkwords connect back to 9:17-18 ("boss," "cautions," "deviant actions"). This is the first formal advice that Qoheleth gives after the frame, and the only advice found in 9:13—10:7. Therefore it may be considered the decisive sentence in the whole unit. Its brevity does not make it unimportant. Once one has achieved a position, one should remain in it as long as possible. "Deviant actions" could refer to one's own actions, namely giving up one's position. But in view of the word links to 9:18 it means rather the deviant actions of the "boss," actions he would take were his last good counselor to leave him.

How acutely contrary to the ironical advice proposed to the fictive courtier in Alexandria in 8:2-4. There, however, the concern was to reveal the fragility of the glory ascribed to a courtier's life in traditional education. In the present context, no secret is made of all that, and yet responsible cooperation is demanded. The leading class, to whom Qoheleth is speaking, must have constantly faced the question whether they should continue to seek political influence, or retreat to commerce and trade and dedicate themselves only to enriching themselves and enjoying life.

[10:5-7] After the "boss," the next subject is his crowd. "Oversight" (a cultic term; see 5:5) is ironic. "Stupidity" is *abstractum pro concreto*. Contrasted with the stupid are, surprisingly, not the cultured but the rich. This shows once again that the intention here is to examine concrete situations in Jerusalem, not to formulate abstract maxims. Already in the Persian period there existed a council of elders, 150 in number, with advisory, if not executive, functions. In it were assembled representatives of the wealthiest families (Neh 5:12; 12:40; 13:11). Later, Antiochus III gave direct political functions as well to this *gerousia*. The criterion of selection was the prominence and wealth of the family. In any case, our text presupposes as self-evident that only the rich could be both knowledgeable and also therefore politically competent. For who else had access to the educational institutions?

But now there was a social upheaval in the upper classes in Jerusalem. In it the old (and only right, even for Qoheleth) system of values was being lost. The process is "evil" (v. 5), just as evil, for example, as a social breakdown that impoverishes rich people and forces them into slavery (5:12—6:6). But Qoheleth's students must know that, if they want to follow the upward track, they cannot count either on the protective power of established groups, or on advancement through real merit and real ability.

Dangers of Upheaval 10:8-11

Ps 7:16; 9:16; 35:8;
57:7; Prov 26:27;
Sir 27:26

8 One who digs a pit can fall into it;
    the one who breaks through a wall, a snake might bite;

9 one who breaks stones can be wounded by them;
   one who splits wood is endangered by that.

10 If the axe has become dull,
    and its user has not sharpened it ahead of time,
    then more muscle power is required—
    he would have drawn profit from knowledge:
    by having prepared his tool in advance.

11 If the snake bites   Sir 12:13
    before he has charmed it,
    the snake charmer
    has no profit.

10:10 Literally: "Knowledge gives the profit of preparing."

Overview of 10:8-11

This piece stands almost without verbal links between 9:13—10:7 on the one hand, and 10:12—11:3 on the other; but this might be due to the fact that very concrete images of daily life are used here. Naturally they demand a specific terminology. There are, however, linkwords back to 9:11-12:

> 10:8   fall
> 10:10   power
>   knowledge

The unit contains six "If . . . then" formulations. The first four (in which the "if" is expressed by a participle in Hebrew—"one who" in translation) are approximately equal in length to the final two (where the "if" is longer, formulated by a sentence, completed by a second negative sentence). The example of the dull axe in v. 10 links associatively with the splitting of wood in v. 9.

Does the unit as a whole perhaps intend to say: whoever undertakes responsible action is threatened by corresponding dangers—but at the same time, through the knowledge gained by education, one can at least render action easier and preclude many mishaps? So, therefore, there is one advantage to education, however limited it may be! But other possible meanings cannot be excluded.

One might also interpret as follows. In all four examples of 10:8-9 one thing is common: something massive and solid is being torn apart, and then danger lurks. Is that possibly a warning against taking part in the social upheaval alluded to earlier? Or was there even an action being prepared against the Ptolemaic leadership in Alexandria, in favor of

Antioch? In this case, 10:8-11 belongs to the text coming in 10:12-20. It would be understandable that the warning should focus on mindless talk. It would have been necessary to encode all this in images, but the recipients at that time would have understood. Unfortunately we have no way of verifying such an interpretive hypothesis. Moreover, Qoheleth not only warns against dangers, but in vv. 10-11 he emphasizes also that knowledge and preparative planning can help. Later, when he warns against talking too much, then certainly he does not appear to be opposed to the undertakings to which he referred.

Notes on 10:8-11

[10:8-9] Verses 8-9 could be formulated: when people are active, they place themselves in danger. For the possible background meaning, see above. It would certainly be wrong to interpret vv. 8-9, on the basis of other recorded sayings about digging holes (Ps 7:15 [MT 16]; 9:15 [MT 16]; 35:8; 57:6 [MT 7]; Prov 26:27; Sir 27:26), as meaning that actions aimed at harming others will strike back at oneself. That fits neither with Qoheleth's rejection of the principle of deeds-consequence relationship, nor with the other three examples.

[10:10-11] Verses 10-11 could assert: with the help of professional skill, used in timely manner, one succeeds better than without it. This is precisely what is affirmed in v. 10b, a bit of the text that bulges beyond the structure of the whole, and that is tied to the whole and given special emphasis through the key word "profit," which recurs in v. 11. We have here probably the original meaning of the word that Qoheleth had long before developed into a philosophical term.

Verse 11 is a saying that is remarkably tightly knit through several rhymes and assonances, not replicable in translation, and in the history of the text it may well have been the nucleus from which all of vv. 8-11 developed.

The Tongue and the Distant King 10:12-20

9:11; Prov 10:32; 15:2; Sir 21:16

    12 Words from the mouth of one who knows are applauded;
        the lips of a fool bring him confusion.
    13 The onset of words from his mouth is foolishness,
        the consequence of his mouth is evil delusion.

5:2; +6:12; 8:7

14 And the ignorant person talks on and on. But humans do not perceive what is about to occur. And what will happen even after that—who can tell?

15 The labor of the foolish will exhaust them, since they do not perceive how to make their way in the city.

16 Woe to you, O land whose king is a slave,
and whose princes feast in the morning

Isa 3:4l; 5:11; Prov 31:4-7

17 Blessed are you, O land whose king is from noble stock
and whose princes schedule their eating
for self-control rather than carousing.

18 If one is slack, the framework sags,
if one drops one's hands, the house leaks.

Prov 20:4

19 One feasts in order to laugh,
and wine gives joy to the living,
and money is involved in both.

2:2
Ps 104:15

20 Even in your thoughts, don't badmouth a king;
even in your bedroom, don't ridicule a wealthy person;
for a bird of the heavens can project your voice,
the winged one can broadcast the words.

Overview of 10:12—11:3

Even though 10:16-17, 20 deal with the king, the nobility, and the wealthy (surrounding the king), the focus has now turned from Jerusalem to Alexandria. But it is Alexandria as a far distant reality. City and country, houses, water, and trees seem to be close at hand. In v. 20 even students from more modest backgrounds (for whom a rich person belongs to a contrasting group), and in v. 15 those whose social advancement could fail, are the ones in view. Verses 8-10 had already brought the most elementary activities of country living to the fore, if primarily in the form of images. From 9:11 it is rather the sentence "bread to the knowledgeable" that is important. Linkwords to 9:11-12 are:

10:12	"knowledgeable"
	"applause"
10:13	"evil"
10:14	"do not perceive"
10:15	"do not perceive"
10:17	"power" (= "self-control" in translation)
10:19	"bread"
10:20	"wealthy"
11:1	"bread"
11:2	"do not perceive"
	"evil"
11:3	"fall" (twice)

At the beginning, 9:11 seems to dominate; 9:12 dominates in the concluding verses of 11:2-3.

The text appears to culminate in the two admonitions of 10:20 and 11:1-2. The first, a warning against careless speech, was prepared by what preceded. The second, a call both to boldness and to caution in commercial affairs, is motivated in the following verse, 11:3.

Notes on 10:12-20

[10:12-14] Verses 12-14 provide a contrast between the knowledgeable and the ignorant in full classical style focusing on the idea that the ignorant harm themselves when they speak. This contrast has a full-dress commentary in Qoheleth's style in v. 14. What is worst is that the ignorant person talks so much. Qoheleth comes after the foolish, now degraded to the ignorant, with combined citations from 8:7 and 6:12. These were originally directed not against the ignorant, but rather against the traditional knowledge and its claim to explain the world. The thought may be that this is true, a fortiori, of the ignorant.

[10:15] Verse 15 is attached to the previous verses by the linkword "foolish." The saying is difficult to interpret and to translate. "Move into the city" may be a proverbial phrase meaning to become rich and to rise socially. Qoheleth's referential group would have consisted predominantly of great landowners, who had, however, long been city dwellers. From there they managed their holdings, did business, and enjoyed life when they took the time for it. But Qoheleth might also have been entrusted with young people from families who had not yet made the leap. If they did not climb upward, but rather fell backward, they would end up doing the hard labor of the land proletariat. So Qoheleth could use this to threaten lazy students.

It is conceivable, however, that in this concrete context the "city" did not mean the city as such, but rather the capital city of the kingdom, Alexandria. The word "city" carries at least the association to which the following verse connects. Probably he had conditions in Alexandria in mind.

[10:16-17] Verses 16-17 are formally a cry of woe and weal over the land, but by their contents focus on king and princes. Whether or not a concrete situation is in view here the original readers would know, but we no longer can. Hebrew *na'ar* can mean either "boy" or "slave." The context would suggest "slave." But it is also possible that Qoheleth is playing here with both meanings. Commentators who propose "boy" usually then refer to Ptolemy V Epiphanes, who ascended the throne in 205 B.C.E., at five years of age, while his guardian, Agathocles, and the latter's sister Agathoclea were creating an uproar by their mismanagement and debauchery. This would allow us to date the book almost to the year. For there was a revolt in 203 B.C.E., and the hated brother and sister were slaughtered by the people of Alexandria. In this interpretation the "king from noble stock" would be identified as Antiochus III, who during these years in Antioch was preparing himself to conquer Palestine. Qoheleth then would be among his secret sympathizers in Jerusalem, and this veiled declaration would be the main point of this part of the text.

[10:18-19] These verses pick up motifs from vv. 16-17: those who begin the day with feasting naturally do not take care of the things that have been entrusted to their care. In v. 18 the "house" can be an image of the state, especially where the Ptolemaic kingdom ideology considered the state as the *oikia,* the household, of the king. In v. 19 "money" could stand for the money that was extorted from the provinces. In this sense the passage could conceal a sharp criticism. Or else, even retaining this contextual sense, the two sayings could have had also a more general meaning: an admonition for the student against laziness and in favor of financial effort, because this is the only path to laughter, to joy.

[10:20] Verse 20 is a return to the theme of "speech," to which perhaps everything from v. 10 on has led. When a revolution is in preparation, then the greatest caution and cunning must rule one's words. The image of the bird is like our expression, "The walls have ears." If the historicizing interpretation of v. 16 is correct, then v. 20 fits in, because Agathocles worked especially hard with information sources and in taking account of denunciations.

Uncertain Future 11:1-3

11:1 Set your bread afloat upon the water,
     for after many days you will find it again.
   2 Divide your capital seven or even eight ways,
     because you do not perceive what evil will occur in the land.
   3 If the clouds swell with rain,
     they will pour it out on the land;
     if a tree falls toward the south, or toward the north,
     wherever the tree falls, that is where it will be.

Overview of 11:1-3

Here the linkwords to 9:11-12 are numerous (see above). These three verses are not only prepared and launched by 9:11-12, but they also build with this text a frame for 9:11—11:3. Especially important is the return of the motif of not knowing. For this now evokes by association the next group of verses, 11:4-8.

In terms of content, the politics of the kingdom is left behind. Qoheleth is once again dealing with the formation of the personal life of his young listeners, which 9:11-12 earlier also had in view. This is another indication that now the frame of the final section of the book will begin.

Notes on 11:1-3

[11:1] The interpretation of the image in v. 1 is difficult. If it is purely an image, it means: you might set up something false with your possessions, through which they would simply be lost—it can happen that thereupon, and directly because of it, they are preserved for you. It belonged to the philosophy of those seeking prosperity in the Hellenistic world to distribute gifts and considerations widely on all sides. Perhaps one day it would pay off. Did Qoheleth mean this? The Jewish tradition had interpreted it mostly in that sense, giving it then, however, a pious turn as a recommendation of almsgiving (see "Make friends for yourself by means of unrighteous mammon," Luke 16:9). Possibly, however, "set your bread upon the water" may have been a conventional image for commerce by sea, evoking naturally a special concern for boldness and risk.

[11:2] The approach presupposed in v. 2 is the greatest caution on the part of the businessperson. Qoheleth provides a motive for each of the approaches, precisely the one that we would give ourselves when deciding for the one or the other. The actual affirmation consists in the paradoxical pairing of the two recommendations. It signifies that no advice can be given. The daring entrepreneur, or the most prudent, can be right. Why?

[11:3] Verse 3a is a "True . . ." sentence: True, there are cases where causal connections can be recognized. To this v. 3b corresponds as a "But . . ." sentence: But there is also the unforeseeable chance event, and what it brings about remains. The connection to v. 2 through the expression "on the land" makes the rain clouds—even though rain is otherwise a blessing—appear here rather as an image of misfortune. The same is true for the trees through the motif of "falling" that by 9:12 is set in the sense of misfortune, if not dying.

Taking Action and Enjoying 11:4-8

4 One who gapes at the blowing air will not sow;
  one who stands observing the clouds will not reap.
5 Just as you cannot perceive the blowing air any more than the development of a child in a pregnant womb, so can you not perceive the action of God, who enacts everything. 6 In the morning begin to plant, and also toward evening do not let your hand rest, since you cannot perceive which will succeed, the one or the other. Or maybe both together will have a happy outcome.

+3:11; +8:17; Ps 139:15

7 Then will the light be sweet,
  and happy for the eyes to see the sun.
8 Because, even when a human being has many years of life,
  one should be joyful in each of them;
  and one should remember the days of darkness:
  they will be many.
  Everything that comes (into the world) is a breath.

11:8 Literally: "that they too will be many."

Overview of 11:4-8

The exhortation toward which this text is heading stands in v. 6: continuously to be active. Qoheleth backs away from concrete advice about how to act (vv. 1-3), but not from the exhortation that act one must! He shifts here from the sphere of the merchant to that of the landowner, but the message is surely valid for both. The basis for the necessity of continuous action is precisely the impossibility of seeing the future (v. 6b, prepared for in vv. 4-5). The key word, translated "happy outcome" (v. 6), links to the outer frame, the command to enjoy life combined with the mention of the "dark days" (vv. 7-8).

   The linkwords, and other linkages, from vv. 4-6 back to vv. 1-3 are so strong that one might also consider a chiastic structure of vv. 1-6:

11:1-2a	exhortation
11:2b-3	invisibility of the future
11:4-5	invisibility of the future
11:6	exhortation

The linkwords are:

11:4	"clouds"	see v. 3
11:5	"pregnant"	see v. 3 (= "swell" in translation)
11:5-6	"perceive"	see v. 2
11:6	"happy outcome"	see v. 2, "evil" (as opposite)

The content of the two exhortations is diverse, however, and vv. 1-3, through their linkages to 9:11-12, also have a clear function as closure to 10:12—11:3. So here, toward the end of the book, we have to reckon with intended interlinking of one end with another beginning (similar to that between vv. 7-8 and 9-10).

Notes on 11:4-8

[11:4] From v. 3 the clouds symbolize the foreseeable; in v. 5 the wind will return as the symbol of the unforeseeable. Verse 4 is in the middle. The two images are compressed together, but something else is intended here: the danger that arises from the need for certainty on the part of those who are oriented toward knowledge. This need of certainty can get to the point that they hold back from acting.

[11:5] "Who enacts everything" means either "who causes both," or it is a statement about universal divine causality (see 3:11 and 8:17). The second is more likely in view of the general argumentation. Here is found, quite casually, one of Qoheleth's most basic theological statements.

[11:7] The verse is connected to what precedes through "and" (literally), which must have the meaning of "then," introducing a consequence—a fact rarely seen by translators and commentators. Verse 6 ends intentionally with *ṭôbîm* ("happy outcome"). This key word is immediately picked up: "It is *happy* for the eyes." The cosmos itself changes when good things from God enter human life. Verse 7, with its few words, throws the reader back into the mood of cosmic fullness and the power of light that was indicated by the introductory hymn in 1:4-11. See Euripides: "Sweet, passing sweet, is light for men to see."[4]

[11:8] The sweetness of the world does not automatically follow from success in human affairs. Joy as a further human activity is interposed. People must appropriate happiness by being joyful and at the same time

---

[4] "Iphigeneia at Aulis," §1252, in *Euripides*, trans. Arthur S. Way, LCL (New York: Macmillan, 1916) 1:115.

reflecting on death—only then will the light be sweet. The thought of death in no way relativizes joy, but rather gives it its strength and justification.

The reader must connect "the dark days" with death in view of what precedes in the book. However, the image is open enough that 12:1-2, which speak of age and illness, can also be linked to it.

The logical connection, success—joy in view of death—cosmic awakening, finds syntactic expression in that a causal clause, beginning "because" (Hebrew *kî*), proceeds in modal verbs. Besides, it commands in the third person. The second-person address begins only in v. 9.

In contrast with the poem from v. 9 on, which begins with joy during one's youth, v. 8 speaks of joy throughout life. Verses 7-8 thus open up, by an anticipatory interpretation, the immediately upcoming poem of closure—at least its opening position, which is modified later within the poem as well. Humans should be joyful as long as they can!

Stylistically, one must notice the repetition of the word "many" in parallelism, and the definition of death as "dark days" versus "light" and "sun," which are the gifts of life. That living is counted in years and death in days is not intended to be significant. These are traditionally paired words for "time." In the last line one could translate "All that comes is a breath." But for Qoheleth it is not the dark days that "come," but rather people (see 1:4). The word "breath," which encapsulates so many analyses of the whole book, is the closing word of the unit 11:4-8. It will recur at the end of the first half of the closing poem (11:10), and then three times more in the concluding sentence of the book, which also ends the closing poem (12:8). Here, as in other particulars, can be seen structures of closure that are analogous to those used in music.

Closing Poem on Joy, Death, and God 11:9—12:8

> 9 Be joyful my boy, in your early days;
> have a happy heart during your boyhood.
> Get along on the paths where your heart leads you,
> toward the visions your eyes put before you.
> [But perceive that God will bring you to judgment for all of that.]
> 10 Keep your mind free of vexation,
> and protect your body from evil,
> for youth and dark hair are a breath.
>
> 12:1 Remember your Creator in your early days,
> prior to when the days of evil come,
> and those years overtake you
> of which you will say: I have no interest in them;

11:9—12:8: 7:1-4

Sir 26:19f

2:10; 6:9

+2:23

2 prior to when the sun and the light and the moon and the
    stars go dark
and the clouds return, even after the rainfall:

3 the day when the guards of the house tremble,
and the strong men are bent,
and the grinders give up, because they are too few,
and the women peering through the windows darken,

4 and the doors on the street are shut;
when the rumble of the mill is muted
the birdsong soars—
all the singers are bowed low;

5 also they fear the exalted one
because terrors lurk on the road;
the almond tree blossoms,
the locust plods along,
the caper berry bursts,
but a human being goes to his eternal home,
and the mourners circle through the streets.

6 Yes, prior to when the silver cord is loosed,
the golden bowl is shattered,
the jar on the well is smashed,
the broken wheel falls into the crater,

+3:20f   7 the dust returns to the earth as it was,
and the air returns to God who gave it.

|| 1:2   8 "A breath, a puff of breath," this man named Qoheleth used to say,
"all are a breath."

11:9 The bracketed prose sentence may not have belonged to the original form of the book.

Overview of 11:9—12:8

This concluding poem, from the point of view of structure, is a "coda" to the closing section of the book, expanding the motives of its outer frame. 12:8 still belongs to the concluding poem, even though it is a frame verse for the whole book.

The poem is most intensively prepared in 11:7-8. The phrases "one should be joyful" and "let them remember" in v. 8 announce the imperatives that organize the poem in its two parts: "Be joyful, my boy" in 11:9 and "Remember your Creator" in 12:1. "Everything that comes is a breath" in 11:8 announces the closing sentences of both parts of the poem in 11:10 and 12:8. Other repeating linkwords are:

"light"	12:2
"happy"	11:9

"eyes"	11:9
"the sun"	12:2, expanded through moon and stars
"years" + "days"	12:1 (and also "days" in 11:9)
"a human being"	12:5
"dark"	12:2, 3
"come"	12:1

The intensity of this linking is unique in the whole book. Within the poem this technique is used less frequently. There are within the poem poetically relevant repetitions only to signal the borders between the two parts of the poem: of the two parallel expressions "youth" and "early days" in 11:9, the first recurs in the last line of the first part (11:10) and the second in the first line of the second part (12:1). Therefore the play of repeated linkwords between 11:7-8 and the poem is meaningful. Now many of the linkwords in 11:7-8 are related to life, but in the poem are related to youth; many that relate to death in the poem are related to illness and to age. Therefore 11:7-8 presents itself as a prior interpretation of the poem.

The structure of the poem itself can be understood only when one perceives how—always in keeping with changes in content—formal expectations are built and then not fulfilled. They are even replaced by unexpected new forms. Syntactically the command to joy is maintained until the end. But death pushes in and grows so strong and overpowering that it covers everything and progressively crowds out the word of joy. A unique situation of poetic uncertainty results. The reader no longer really knows what the theme was: a call to enjoy life during youth or a reflection on death. Into this indecision of understanding there falls as the last word, with full voice, the word "God."

The first half, 11:9-10, builds on—certainly not in monotonous, but still in strict, form—a classical literary structure in the style of Hebrew poetry. Dominant are the imperatives: "Be joyful" and "have a happy heart" (first parallelism). This is made explicit in the search for joy ("Get along" with double object: second parallelism), and in avoiding evil ("keep free" and "protect": third parallelism, extended by a motive sentence that ends the whole).

We now expect an analogous structure in the second half, which—corresponding to the theme announcement in 11:8—clearly begins in 12:1. But here surprises begin. We expect "Remember death" or "Remember darkness." But we get "Remember your Creator." A trick to confuse the reader? A *ritardando*? An instinctive avoidance of the real

theme? Then we wait for the parallel. By analogy with the beginning in
11:9, there should be a second imperative (parallel to "Remember") and
a second time specification (parallel to "early days"). There is no second
imperative. It can be dropped if the time specification has been amplified,
and that is the case here (it is apparently even necessitated because the
parallel word "youth" has been used up in 11:10 as a motif of closure).
The time specification is a temporal clause introduced by "prior to." But
now a floodgate is opened. The time setting "prior to" suddenly now
opens the indirect possibility of speaking about illness, age, and death,
and this happens so strongly that all the remainder of the poem, long as it
is, is based on this specification of time, on this ending of the second half
of the first parallelism. The formal means of this volcanic outbreak is suc-
cessive dividing.

As 12:2 begins, "prior to" has hanging on it only one parallelism,
metrically grown quite long. But then v. 2 sets up parallel to it with
another "prior to." The parallelism that is naturally required here is
extended in v. 3 by "the day," and at that point the subordinate-clause status of the whole is almost forgotten, and an independent image of age is
developed. Suddenly, with its classical series of marked parallels, this
meets the enduring expectations of the first part of the poem, even though
not when expected. In the middle of this measured flow of parallelisms
the connection is abruptly broken, where the second stich of v. 4, through
a temporal subordinate clause ("when the rumble of the mill is muted"),
introduces a completely independent description that, at the same time,
signifies a transition from the foregoing allegory to the direct description
of a day of death. An introductory *gam,* "also," in v. 5 raises this description toward its peak, which is reached finally at the end of v. 5. The
description was built, at least in v. 5, as an antithesis: here nature bursting
with life, there the funeral procession and the mourners. With this is
reached an initial resting place.

Precisely here it is possible to refer back to the earlier extended
suspension. For the third time there occurs "prior to" (v. 6), and now
there follows a sixfold definition of death that once again meets the
expectations of classical form at an unexpected point, thus bringing final
closure: four times in metaphors, twice in anthropological-theological
formulas, which, what is more, recall for this purpose the beginning of
the Bible. Also put to rest is the question that remained troubling about
the unexpected mention of the word "Creator" in 12:1.

The restructuring of content and form within the poem, and also
the discrepancy between the introduction (11:7-8) and the poem itself, at

least its beginning, can best be explained as follows: Qoheleth is in no way of the opinion that young people should enjoy life because old age looks gloomy. Such can be read, of course, in Greek authors. But his teaching is that each one should be joyful at all times, if this is given to one, and that always in view of death. His message could clearly be mis-read, however, to yield a different sense in a cultural milieu under Greek influence. So he starts his song in keeping with this other sense, but then allows it to fall apart and transform itself into his own message. To make this absolutely clear, he also places before his poem an introduction that points right off in the direction of his definitive message. Qoheleth dis-sembles his voice when he instructs the young to rejoice in view of old age and illness. That is precisely what he wants to take them away from.

Notes on 11:9—12:8

[11:9] The prose insert may originate with the author of the second post-script (12:13-14); compare the similar, and otherwise rare, formulation in 12:14. The addition intends to protect the text from a libertine interpreta-tion. Whether a next-worldly judgment of the dead is thought of is not entirely clear. It is rather unlikely. For in that case the book's statements about death as the radical end for each person would similarly have required an appropriate correction. For the context of this gloss see the surmise on pp. 11–13.

[12:1] In the Hebrew text the effect of "Creator" is somewhat more sub-tle than indicated above. The word is in the plural, surely as a plural of majesty (which is, however, unusual). Moreover, it sounds very similar to the word translated as "crater," an open pit, which again is commonly an image of the underworld and of death. This word occurs in v. 6. As the spelling in v. 1 is unusual, there probably, in the one word, both words could be recognized at the same time. The reader of v. 1 expects "death" but hears at first "crater," then realizes that "Creator" was what was said. At the end of the poem, this "Creator" is doubly recalled: through "crater" (v. 6) and "God" (v. 7).

[12:2] Into the normal triad "sun, moon, and stars" there is inserted the "light," recalling 11:7 and prolonging the view as in a long leave-taking. After rain in Palestine one normally has brilliant blue skies immediately. So something abnormal is described. The reader would be reminded of the prophetic, and possibly already the apocalyptic, topos of end-time catastrophes. Qoheleth here takes this theme down into an individual life.

Thus the darkening of heavenly lights, and the lingering darkness even during the day, can be related to the slow loss of sight of older people. Here begins something like an allegorical treatment of the empirical world.

[12:3] Now he is fully there. The house, which comes to rest in the evening, means the body with its various parts: arms, legs, teeth, eyes, mouth, ears. The comparison of the human body with a house, of arms with guards, and teeth with millstones is also found in Greek texts. Women grinders, in the ancient Near East, were house servants who turned handmills. The meaning of many of the expressions is easily understood: "tremble," "bent," "too few." The persons who appear are in precise order: first men, then women (in Hebrew "grinders" is feminine plural), each time first the servers, then the owners (instead of "strong men" one could also translate "noblemen," instead of "women" also "noblewomen"). Beneath the allegory, by the same token, are to be recognized the inhabitants of a house where catastrophe has occurred. In this pairing of image and reality lies the secret of these lines.

[12:4-5] Regarding the ears in v. 4, however, there is no mention of an object in the house. Still the allegory remains through the "rumble of the mill." Besides, a transition occurs in this "when" clause from allegory to direct description of dying and death. The text here can be interpreted and translated in very different ways.

According to many translations, there begins at the end of v. 4 a characterizing of old age. Sleep at night is light and brief. Early, when the first birds twitter, the elderly wake up, but the birdsong is lost on ears growing deaf. The anxiety of old people about going out of the house, with all the possible complications this can entail (beginning of v. 5), imperceptibly leads the imagination from the old people into nature. A nature full of vitality and fertility is evoked by the almond tree, the locust, the caper berry, and then suddenly the old person is again in view: now dead and being carried to the grave. "Eternal home" is a fixed symbol for the grave.

According to our translation, the description of the house threatened by terror, which was the basis for the allegory on aging, now as such comes to the fore in v. 4. One learns gradually—it is clear only at the end of v. 5—that a person has died in the house. When the daily noises grow quiet, suddenly the birdsong, which has always been there, becomes audible. We see women singers bowing low. That is the beginning of the grieving. The singers are anxious. Who is "the exalted one" whom they fear, when now they take the road (to the burial)? Death? God? Then comes the contrary image: overflowing nature, and finally the funeral cortege.

[**12:6**] The first two images may refer to a lamp that hangs as a bowl from the ceiling. Decisive are the precious materials: silver and gold. Also water from springs is costly. In the wheel we must see a wheel over a well, upon which runs a rope with a bucket. These technical novelties were introduced in Palestine only in the third century. From image to image the words have carried associations to that image which constantly unites grave, underworld, and death together, that is, the pit of darkness.

[**12:7**] With all the solemnity and the enrichment through theological dimension in this text, this sober definition of death also serves to block out all the mythical elements concerning death imagined in connection with "eternal home" and with "grave." Death as end, in this context, is univocal. The point of view, no doubt polemical, in 3:21 is far away. Therefore, when here it is said, as taken for granted, that the air of breath returns to God, this is hardly in disagreement with 3:21.

[**12:8**] The verse belongs to the poem; see 11:10 and, earlier, 11:8. But by the same token it is the frame verse to the whole book. It shows no longer the fully developed three-step parallelism of 1:2. Such emphasis on something still unknown, just being introduced, is no longer needed here at the end. In the interim the clause has enriched itself with a bookful of reflections, and it needs now only to be heard in a whisper to evoke an echo in the reader.

Epilogue

First Postscript: 12:9-11

9 Qoheleth was a man of knowledge. But even more: he taught the people the art of perception. He listened, and tested, and he straightened out many a proverb. 10 Qoheleth sought to find interesting sayings, and these true sayings are here painstakingly recorded.

11 The sayings of those who know are like goads,
   like driven pegs are the words of writers of collections—
   both are wielded by one and the same shepherd.

Overview of 12:9-11

This postscript provides information about the author and his book. Its language derives from Qoheleth and yet comes from another hand. A surmise concerning the occasion and purpose of this postscript is to be found in the Introduction, pp. 11–13.

Notes on 12:9-11

[12:9] An attempt to make education available to simple folk, or even the unrestricted offering of teaching to the general public, must have been something new or unusual—otherwise it would not have been so emphasized. If the call of Wisdom through the streets and marketplaces in Proverbs 1–9 had the same meaning, we would almost have to suppose that these chapters were dated no earlier. The wording "to teach the people recalls 2 Chron 17:9. Possibly there was no other Hebrew expression for peripatetic teaching.

In "listen" and "tested" (v. 9) we may see a veiled indication that Qoheleth has opened up a completely new (i.e., Greek) cultural tradition. By "he straightened out many a proverb" we are led to think of those parts of the book in which Qoheleth disputes the traditional wisdom ideology, most of which appears in the form of sayings. For "straightened out" see 1:15; 7:13.

[12:10] Verse 10 turns to the writing down of Qoheleth's teaching. Since the book's narrator presents the wise Qoheleth as a voice cited by himself, looking back, the book could be considered as one not written by Qoheleth at all. This is the only adequate explanation of the passive formulation at the end of v. 10. This tells us nothing about the real authorship. Qoheleth may have simply hidden himself behind a fictive editor. But also someone else may have put the book together based on Qoheleth's materials. It is not likely that the book consists of several separate collections, one superimposed on the other. Until now, no theory attempting to show a variety of hands at work in the history of the book's composition has proven to be convincing.

[12:11] As often occurs in Qoheleth, v. 11 brings closure by a saying. It deals with the effect of sayings collections. But its function in the context is to affirm, as taken for granted, that the Qoheleth book falls within the category *(Gattung)* of sayings collection. The first two lines of the saying, by the comparisons they introduce, note opposed effects. Proverbs in collections have a dynamic effect, they drive forward—at the same time they serve as nails or pegs to hold and stabilize. Remaining with the image, the third line says that every shepherd intends both of these effects in dealing with his animals. Thus why should sayings collections not be both progressive and conservative? The traditional interpretation of this saying presumed a translation "they are the gift of a single shepherd," and referred the affirmation either to Solomon or to God himself.

Second Postscript 12:12-14

12 From more collections, my son, be warned. Even if there is never an end to the activity of making book after book; and much study ruins one's health 13 after all has been heard, the final word would only be:

Fear God and keep his commandments!
For that is everything for humankind. 14 For God brings every activity to judgment, every hidden thing, whether good or evil.

Sir 43:27

3:14; 5:6; 7:18; 8:12; Deut 5:29; 6:2; 8:6; 10:12f; 13:5; 17:19; 31:12; Sir 1:11-30

to 12:14: 11:9

Notes on 12:12-14

[12:12] This second postscript considers the reader as a normal student ("my son"). It starts by making the case against the preparing of new books (textbooks?), and perhaps even against the overburdening of students through ever more extensive textbooks.

[12:13-14] Verses 13-14, probably in the face of criticisms, reduce the book of Qoheleth (which one "hears" rather than "reads"!) to a simple orthodox formula, which originates in Deuteronomy. See also 11:9. The formula does not do justice to the book, but may well have helped it at that time, and given direction for its interpretation long after.

[12:14] In this regard v. 14 even seizes on an important aspect of Qoheleth's teaching: that we humans do not see to the bottom of things ("every hidden thing").

A surmise about the occasion and purpose of this second postscript is to be found in the Introduction, pp. 12–13.

Select Bibliography

1. Other Publications about Qoheleth by Norbert Lohfink

Lohfink, Norbert. "Les épilogues du livre de Qohélet et les débuts du Canon." In *"Ouvrir les Écritures": Mélanges offerts à Paul Beauchamp à l'occasion de ses soixante-dix ans*, ed. Pietro Bovati and Roland Meynet. LeDiv 162. Paris: Cerf, 1995. 77–96.

———. " 'Freu dich, junger Mann. . . .': Das Schlußgedicht des Koheletbuches (Koh 11,9—12,8)." *BiKi* 45 (1990) 12–19.

———. "Gegenwart und Ewigkeit. Die Zeit im Buch Kohelet." *GuL* 60 (1987) 2–12.

———. "Ist Kohelets hebel-Aussage erkenntnistheoretisch gemeint?" In *Qohelet in the Context of Wisdom*. Ed. A. Schoors. BETL 136. Leuven: Peeters, 1998. 41–59.

———. "Das Koheletbuch: Strukturen und Struktur." In *Das Buch Kohelet: Studien zur Struktur, Geschichte, Rezeption und Theologie*. Ed. L. Schwienhorst-Schönberger. BZAW 254; Berlin: de Gruyter, 1997. 39–121.

———. "Das 'Poikilometron': Kohelet und Menippos von Gadara." *BiKi* 45 (1990) 19.

———. "Qoheleth 5:17-19: Revelation by Joy." *CBQ* 52 (1990) 625–35.

———. *Studien zu Kohelet*. SBAB 26. Stuttgart: Katholisches Bibelwerk, 1998. [12 collected scholarly essays. Their titles are not shown in the essays listed here.]

———. "Technik und Tod nach Kohelet." In *Strukturen christlicher Existenz: FS Friedrich Wulf*, ed. Heinrich Schlier, 27–35. Würzburg: Echter, 1968.

———. "Von Windhauch, Gottesfurcht und Gottes Antwort in der Freude." *BiKi* 45 (1990) 26–32.

———. "Der Weise und das Volk in Koh 12,9 und Sir 37,23." In *Treasures of Wisdom: Studies in Ben Sira and the Book of Wisdom*. Ed. N.

Calduch-Benages and J. Vermeylen. BETL 143. Leuven: Peeters, 1999. 405–10.

———. "Zu einigen Satzeröffnungen im Epilog des Koheletbuches." In *"Jedes Ding hat seine Zeit. . . .": Studien zur israelitischen und altorientalischen Weisheit: 1 Diethelm Michel zum 65. Geburtstag*. Ed. A. A. Diesel. Berlin: de Gruyter, 1996. 131–47.

2. Commentaries

Bergant, Dianne. *Ecclesiastes*. OTM 18. Wilmington, Del.: Glazier, 1982.

Brown, William P. *Ecclesiastes*. IBC. Louisville: Westminster John Knox, 2000.

Crenshaw, James L. *Ecclesiastes: A Commentary*. OTL. Philadelphia: Westminster, 1987.

Delitzsch, Franz. *Proverbs, Ecclesiastes, Song of Solomon*. In *Commentary on the Old Testament in Ten Volumes* by C. F. Keil and F. Delitzsch. Volume 6. Translated by James Martin. Grand Rapids: Eerdmans, 1980.

Fox, Michael V. *A Time to Tear Down and a Time to Build Up: A Rereading of Ecclesiastes*. Grand Rapids: Eerdmans, 1999.

Ginsburg, Christian D. *Coheleth, Commonly Called the Book of Ecclesiastes*. London: Longman, 1861. Reprint: *The Song of Songs and Coheleth*. New York: KTAV, 1971.

Gordis, Robert. *Koheleth: The Man and his World*. 3d ed. New York: Schocken, 1968.

Hertzberg, Hans Wilhelm. *Der Prediger. Das Buch Esther*. 2d ed. KAT 17. Gütersloh: Mohn, 1963.

Japhet, Sara, and Robert B. Salters, editors and translators. *The Commentary of R. Samuel ben Meir, Rashbam, on Qoheleth*. Leiden: Brill, 1985.

Krüger, Thomas. *Qoheleth*. Translated by O. C. Dean Jr. Hermeneia. Minneapolis: Fortress Press, forthcoming. (German ed. 2000.)

Lauha, Aarre. *Koheleth*. BK 19. Neukirchen-Vluyn: Neukirchener, 1978.

Leiman, Harold I. *Koheleth: Life and Its Meaning. A Modern Translation and Interpretation of the Book of Ecclesiastes*. New York: Feldheim, 1978.

Levy, Ludwig. *Das Buch Qoheleth: Ein Beitrag zur Geschichte des Sadduzäismus*. Leipzig: Hinrich, 1912.

Longman, Tremper III. *The Book of Ecclesiastes*. NICOT. Grand Rapids: Eerdmans, 1998.

Murphy, Roland E. *Ecclesiastes*. WBC 23A. Dallas: Word, 1992.

————. *Wisdom Literature: Job, Proverbs, Ruth, Canticles, Ecclesiastes, and Esther.* FOTL 13. Grand Rapids: Eerdmans, 1981.

Podechard, Emmanuel. *L'Ecclésiaste.* EtB. Paris: Gabalda, 1912.

Scott, R. B. Y. *Proverbs, Ecclesiastes.* AB 18. Garden City, N.Y.: Doubleday, 1965.

Seow, C. L. *Ecclesiastes: A New Translation with Introduction and Commentary.* AB 18C. New York: Doubleday, 1997.

Towner, W. Sibley. "The Book of Ecclesiastes: Introduction, Commentary, and Reflections." In *The New Interpreter's Bible,* vol. 5, 265–370. Nashville: Abingdon, 1997.

Whybray, R. N. *Ecclesiastes.* NCBC. Grand Rapids: Eerdmans, 1989.

Zimmerli, Walther. *Prediger.* 2d ed. ATD 16. Göttingen: Vandenhoeck & Ruprecht, 1980.

3. Studies

Bickermann, Elias. *Four Strange Books of the Bible: Jonah, Daniel, Koheleth, Esther.* New York: Schocken, 1967.

Braun, Rainer. *Kohelet und die frühhellenistische Popularphilosophie.* BZAW 130. Berlin: de Gruyter, 1973.

Brown, William P. "'Whatever Your Hand Finds to Do': Qoheleth's Work Ethic." *Int* 55 (2001) 271–84.

Castellino, G. R. "Qohelet and His Wisdom." *CBQ* 30 (1968) 15–28.

Christianson, Eric S. *A Time to Tell: Narrative Strategies in Ecclesiastes.* JSOTSup 280. Sheffield: Sheffield Academic Press, 1998.

Crenshaw, James L. "Ecclesiastes." In *ABD* 2.271–80.

————. "The Eternal Gospel (Eccl. 3:11)." In *Essays in Old Testament Ethics: J. Philip Hyatt, In Memoriam,* edited by James L. Crenshaw and John T. Willis, 22–55. New York: Ktav, 1974.

Crüsemann, Frank. "The Unchangeable World: The 'Crisis of Wisdom' in Koheleth." In *The God of the Lowly: Socio-Historical Interpretations of the Bible,* edited by Willy Schottroff and Wolfgang Stegemann, translated by Matthew J. O'Connell, 57–77. Maryknoll, N.Y.: Orbis, 1984.

————. "Hiob und Kohelet." In *Werden und Wirken des Alten Testaments: Festschrift für Claus Westermann,* edited by Rainer Albertz et al., 373–93. Göttingen: Vandenhoeck & Ruprecht, 1980.

Dahood, Mitchell J. "Canaanite-Phoenician Influence in Qoheleth." *Bib* 33 (1952) 30–52.

Dulin, Rachel Z. "'How Sweet is the Light': Qoheleth's Age-Centered Teachings." *Int* 55 (2001) 260–70.

Bibliography

Fischer, Alexander Achilles. *Skepsis oder Furcht Gottes? Studien zur Komposition und Theologie des Buches Kohelet.* BZAW 247. New York: de Gruyter, 1997.

Fox, Michael V. *Qoheleth and His Contradictions.* JSOTSup 71. Sheffield: Sheffield Academic Press, 1989.

———. "Qoheleth's Epistemology." *HUCA* 58 (1987) 137–55.

Gianto, Agustinus. "The Theme of Enjoyment in Qoheleth." *Bib* 73 (1992) 528–32.

Ginsberg, H. L. "The Quintessence of Koheleth." In *Biblical and Other Studies,* edited by A. Altmann, 47–59. Cambridge: Harvard Univ. Press, 1963.

Good, Edwin M. *Irony in the Old Testament.* Philadelphia: Westminster, 1965.

Gordis, Robert. *Koheleth: The Man and His World. A Study of Ecclesiastes.* 3d ed. New York: Schocken, 1968.

———. "Qoheleth and Qumran—A Study of Style." *Bib* 41 (1960) 395–410.

Hengel, Martin. *Judaism and Hellenism: Studies in Their Encounter in Palestine during the Early Hellenistic Period.* 2 vols. Translated by John Bowden. Philadelphia: Fortress Press, 1974.

Horton, E. "Koheleth's Concept of Opposites." *Numen* 19 (1972) 1–21.

Kaiser, Otto. "Qoheleth." In *Wisdom in Ancient Israel: Essays in Honour of J. A. Emerton,* edited by John Day et al., 83–93. Cambridge: Cambridge Univ. Press, 1995.

Kugel, James L. "Qoheleth and Money." *CBQ* 51 (1989) 32–49.

Levine, Etan. "The Humor in Qohelet." *ZAW* 109 (1997) 71–83.

Loader, John A. *Polar Structures in the Book of Qoheleth.* BZAW 152. Berlin: de Gruyter, 1979.

Loretz, Oswald. *Qoheleth und der Alte Orient: Untersuchungen zu Stil und theologischer Thematik des Buches Qohelet.* Freiburg: Herder, 1964.

Michaud, R. *Qohélet et l'hellénisme.* Paris: Cerf, 1987.

Michel, Diethelm. *Qohelet.* Erträge der Forschung 258. Darmstadt: Wissenschaftliche Buchgesellschaft, 1988.

———. *Untersuchungen zur Eigenart des Buches Qohelet.* BZAW 183. Berlin: de Gruyter, 1989. [With complete Bibliography on Qoheleth 1875–1989 by R. G. Lehmann.]

Murphy, Roland E. "Qoheleth and Theology." *BTB* 21 (1991) 30–33.

———. "The Sage in Ecclesiastes and Qoheleth the Sage." In *The Sage in Israel and the Ancient Near East,* edited by John G. Gammie and Leo G. Perdue, 263–71. Winona Lake, Ind.: Eisenbrauns, 1990.

Ogden, Graham S. "The 'Better'-Proverb (Tôb-Spruch), Rhetorical Criticism, and Qoheleth." *JBL* 96 (1977) 489–505.

———. Qoheleth XI 7—XII 8: Qoheleth's Summons to Enjoyment and Reflection." *VT* 34 (1984) 27–38.

———. "Qoheleth's Use of the 'Nothing Is Better' Form." *JBL* 98 (1979) 339–50.

Palm, August. *Die Qohelet-Literatur: Ein Beitrag zur Geschichte der Exegese des Alten Testaments.* Mannheim: Hogrefe, 1886. [Full Bibliography until 1886.]

Priest, John. "Humanism, Skepticism, and Pessimism in Israel." *JAAR* 36 (1968) 311–26.

Rad, Gerhard von. *Wisdom in Israel.* Translated by James D. Martin. Nashville: Abingdon, 1972.

Rose, Martin. *Rien de nouveau: Nouvelles approches du livre de Qohéleth, avec une bibliographie (1988–1998).* OBO 168. Göttingen: Vandenhoeck & Ruprecht, 1999.

Salters, Robert B. "Qoheleth and the Canon." *ExpT* 86 (1975) 339–42.

Schoors, Antoon. *The Preacher Sought to Find Pleasing Words: A Study of the Language of Qoheleth.* Orientalia Lovaniensia Analecta 41. Leuven: Peeters, 1992.

———, ed. *Qohelet in the Context of Wisdom.* BETL 136. Leuven: Peeters, 1998.

Schwienhorst-Schönberger, Ludger. *"Nicht im Menschen gründet das Glück" (Kohl 2,24): Kohelet im Spannungsfeld jüdischer Weisheit und hellenistischer Philosophie.* HBS 2. Freiburg: Herder, 1994.

———, ed. *Das Buch Kohelet: Studien zur Struktur, Geschichte, Rezeption und Theologie.* BZAW 254. Berlin: de Gruyter, 1997.

Seow, C. L. "Beyond Mortal Grasp: The Usage of *Hebel* in Ecclesiastes." *ABR* 48 (2000) 1–16.

———. "The Socioeconomic Context of 'The Preacher's' Hermeneutic." *PSB* 17 (1996) 168–95.

———. "Theology When Everything Is Out of Control." *Int* 55 (2001) 237–49.

Sheppard, Gerald T. "The Epilogue to Qoheleth as Theological Commentary." *CBQ* 39 (1977) 182–89.

Tamez, Elsa. "Ecclesiastes: A Reading from the Periphery." *Int* 55 (2001) 250–59.

Bibliography

Whitley, Charles F. *Koheleth: His Language and Thought.* BZAW 148. Berlin: de Gruyter, 1979.

Whybray, R. N. *Ecclesiastes.* OTG. Sheffield: JSOT Press, 1989.

———. "Qoheleth, Preacher of Joy." *JSOT* 23 (1982) 87–98.

Williams, James G. "What Does It Profit a Man? The Wisdom of Koheleth." *Judaism* 20 (1971) 179–93.

Wright, Addison G. "The Riddle of the Sphinx: The Structure of the Book of Qoheleth." *CBQ* 30 (1968) 313–34.

———. "The Riddle of the Sphinx Revisited: Numerical Patterns in the Book of Qoheleth." *CBQ* 42 (1980) 38–51.

Zimmerli, Walther. "Das Buch Kohelet—Traktat oder Sentenzensammlung?" *VT* 24 (1974) 221–30.

Index of Ancient Sources

Note: This index does not include the marginal cross-references or references to Qoheleth within the related commentary section.

151

Ancient Sources

Ancient Sources

Index of Subjects

breath, 2, 36, 46, 47, 51, 53, 54, 57, 66, 69, 70, 71, 75, 81, 83, 106, 120, 135, 136

canon, 3, 11–13, 14–17

death, 2, 15, 16, 44,48, 54, 56, 65, 68, 83, 85, 87, 88, 93, 96, 103, 106, 112, 113, 114, 133, 135, 137, 138, 139, 140, 141
deed-consequence relationship, 2, 16, 90, 96, 105, 107, 110

eternal return, 16, 41, 61
evil, 61, 82, 83, 106, 107, 126, 134
existentialism, viii, 14, 62, 45, 54, 110

fear of God, 2, 9, 13, 17, 62, 75, 97, 98, 108, 110, 112

happiness, joy, xiv, 3, 44, 45, 46, 50, 51, 54, 56, 59, 60, 62, 65, 70, 83, 84, 85, 93, 106, 110, 113, 114, 120, 133, 134, 135, 136, 137

Hellenistic background, viii, ix, 4–7, 10–11, 11–13, 14–15, 40, 46, 50, 51, 64, 69, 80, 86, 90, 99, 100, 117–119, 130, 131, 132, 141, 142

it happens, 55, 82

literary criticism, viii, ix, 7, 8, 13–14, 35–36, 46, 55, 56, 59–60
linkword, xiii, 7, 45, 48, 76, 81, 92, 123, 127, 129, 130, 132, 134, 136, 137

observe, 65–66, 68, 69, 72, 73, 100, 124

perfect, 2, 15, 61, 77, 85

Solomon, 12, 14, 35, 44, 45, 56, 58, 59, 64, 143

teacher, 1, 10, 17, 48, 142
traditional wisdom, 2, 3, 5, 6,12, 13, 72, 89–91, 92, 94, 95, 99, 100, 101, 108, 117, 130, 142
translation, vii–xi, xii–xv, 3, 47, 49, 67

Index of Ancient Authors and Groups

Index of Greek Words and Phrases

Index of Hebrew Words and Phrases